101 Life Skills for Teen Girls

How to Be Confident, Find a job, Fix your Car, Make Friends, Manage Time, Be Healthy and Everything Else Teenage girl Should Know Before 18.

By

Kardas Publishing

© Copyright 2023 by Kardas Publishing - All rights reserved.

Without the prior written permission of the Publisher, no part of this publication may be stored in a retrieval system, replicated, or transferred in any form or medium, digital, scanning, recording, printing, mechanical, or otherwise, except as permitted under 1976 United States Copyright Act, section 107 or 108. Permission concerns should be directed to the publisher's permission department.

Legal Notice

This book is copyright protected. It is only to be used for personal purposes. Without the author's or publisher's permission, you cannot paraphrase, quote, copy, distribute, sell, or change any part of the information in this book.

This book is written and published independently. Please keep in mind that the material in this publication is solely for educational and entertaining purposes. All efforts have provided authentic, up-to-date, trustworthy, and comprehensive information. There are no express or implied assurances. The purpose of this book's material is to assist readers in having a better understanding of the subject matter. The activities, information, and exercises are provided solely for self-help information. This book is not intended to replace expert psychologists, legal, financial, or other guidance. If you require counseling, please get in touch with a qualified professional.

By reading this text, the reader accepts that the author will not be held liable for any damages, indirectly or directly, experienced due to the use of the information included herein, particularly, but not limited to, omissions, errors, or inaccuracies. As a reader, you are accountable for your decisions, actions, and consequences.

Table of Content

Introduction...8

Chapter 1: You are Swiss Cheese! Top Tier and Full of Holes...........................12

1.1 Navigating the Emotion Compass..14
- How to Understand Your Emotions?...14
- How to Act on Your Emotions?..16

1.2 A Journey to Self-love and Self-Confidence..17
- How to Love Yourself?..18
- How to Develop Self-Esteem and Self-Confidence?..................................19
- How to Deal with Bullying?..21
- How to be Sexually Educated?...22
- How to deal with Body Image Issues?...23
- How to Avoid Peer Pressure?..24

1.3 Building Meaningful Relationships..25
- How to Make Friends?..26
- How to Avoid Drama and Deal with Fights?..27
- How to Approach Someone You Like?..28

1.4 Learning to Cope..30
- How to Meditate?...30
- How to Problem Solve?..31

Chapter 2: Let that Body do the Talking..32

2.1 Taking Care of the Inside..33
- How to Choose Healthy Food and Drinks?...33
- How to have the Best Sleep?...35
- How to Read the Nutrition Food Label?...36
- How to Choose Your Food Portion?..37
- How to Get Enough Exercise?...37
- How to Take Care of Your Skin?..38
- How to Take Care of Your Hair?..39
- How to Stay Hygienic?..40

2.2 Taking Care of the Outside...42
- How to Pick Under Clothes?..42
- How to Pick Bottoms?..43
- How to Pick Tops?..44
- How to Pick Dresses?...44
- How to Pick Shoes?..44
- How to Dress Smartly?...45
- How to Dress for a Job Interview?..46
- How to Shop Wisely?..47

Chapter 3: Nothing Hotter than being Self-Sufficient...49

3.1 Domestic Skills..50

- How to Shop for Groceries? Make a List of Items You Need...............................51
- How to Cook Simple Meals?...52
- How to Do Laundry?..53
- How to Tidy Up Your Room?..53
- How to Hang a Picture?...54
- How to Clear a Clogged Sink?...55
- How to Unclog a Toilet?...56
- How to Deal with a Fire at Home?..56

3.2 Technical Skills...57

- How to Schedule a Doctor's Appointments?..58
- How to Take the Bus?..59
- How to Defend Yourself?...60
- How to Use First AID?..61
- How to Communicate Well?..62

Chapter 4: Eyes on the Prize Champ!..65

- 4.1 How to Set Goals?...66
- 4.2 How to Manage Time?..67
- 4.3 How to Organize?..68
- 4.4 How to Improve Your Memory?..70
- 4.5 How to Multitask and be Good at It?..71
- 4.6 How to be Self-Resistant?...73
- 4.7 How to Concentrate?..74
- 4.8 How to Manage Stress?..76
- 4.9 How to Cope with Failure?..77
- 4.10 How to Boost Cognitive Flexibility?..79
- 4.11 How to Visualize?...80
- 4.12 How to be Productive?..81
- 4.13 How to Find Your Inner Zen?...83

Chapter 5: Pack Your Bag for a Better Future..85

- 5.1 How to Find a College?...86
- 5.2 How to Know the Cost of Moving Out?..87
- 5.3 What You Need to Consider When Making a Budget?...................................89
- 5.4 How to Make a Realistic Budget?..91
- 5.5 What to Pack for Living in a Dorm or an Apartment?.....................................92
- 5.6 How to Find an Apartment?..94

5.7 What You Need to Know When Sharing with Flat mates?...96

5.8 What You Need to Know about Living in a Dorm?...97

5.9 How to Build Your Credit?...99

5.10 How to Deal with Homesickness?..100

5.11 How to Cope with Challenges in the Dorm?..101

5.12 How to Build Boundaries?..102

Chapter 6: Hunt for the Dollar in Your Pocket...105

6.1 How to Create a CV?...106

6.2 How to Find a Job?..107

6.3 How to Fill Out a Job Application?..108

6.4 How to Develop Employability Skills?..109

6.5 How to Prepare for a Job Interview?...110

6.6 How to Manage Money?..112

6.7 What is there to Learn about Personal Banking?..113

6.8 How to Find Side Gigs?..114

6.9 How to Develop a Healthy Relationship with Money?..115

6.10 What You Need to Know about Your Taxes?..116

6.11 How to Invest Your Money?..117

6.12 How to Avoid Debt?...119

6.13 How to Get Your Bills in Order?...120

6.14 How to Get Free Stuff?...120

Chapter 7: Your Four Wheels on the Black Carpet...122

7.1 How to Set Your Car Buying Budget?..123

7.2 How to Find the Right Car?..124

7.3 Should You Get a Used or New Car?...125

7.4 How to Pay for Your Car?...125

7.5 How to Negotiate at the Dealership?..126

7.6 How to Practice Road Safety?..127

7.7 How to Practice Basic Car Maintenance?..129

7.8 What to Do If Your Car Breaks Down?..130

7.9 How to Navigate Your Ways?..132

7.10 How to Keep Your Car Clean?..133

Chapter 8: When Surfing the Web Waters 136

8.1 How to Make Sure Your Internet Connection is Secure? 137
8.2 How to Use the Internet Mindfully? 137
8.3 How to Check if a Link is Safe? 138
8.4 How to Choose Strong Passwords? 139
8.5 How to Recognize an Online Predator? 140
8.6 What to Do When You Get Hacked? 142
8.7 How to Identify When You are Being Catfished? 144
8.8 How to Shop Online Mindfully? 146
8.9 How to Protect Your Privacy on Social Media? 147
8.10 What to Have Fun on the Internet and Be Safe? 149

Roadmap for a Happy Life 152

A FREE PRINTABLE GIFT TO OUR READERS!

Print it at home!

Get FREE, unlimited access to it and all our new books by joining our community!

SCAN WITH YOUR CAMERA TO JOIN!

Introduction

Congratulations, you have made it! You are a teen!

The teenage years are undoubtedly the most awkward, difficult, and stressful years of your life. Being a teenager might be the most difficult time in your life. You are currently at a stage where you are attempting to define who you are, both to those around you and yourself.

This stage bursts with hope, energy, life, beauty, and passion. It is a time to attempt new things, fail, learn, and grow and a bridge to adulthood. Most teens dread adulthood.

When I was a teenager, the story was no different. I wanted to grow up, but I was not really a fan of everything that came with it. I spent my days mindlessly trying to shut out all my worries and fears. At one end, I was worried that I had no plans for my future; at another, I felt too overwhelmed to make any. It was a vicious cycle. It seemed everybody was pulling me from all different directions. Amidst all the expectations, I was too confused to even think if I wanted something. There seemed a lot of disparity between being what everyone thought to be the best and being myself.

When you have so much to figure out and are not equipped with the right skills, it makes everything ten times more difficult. Life skills are basically your survival guide!

You must know by now that the teenage years are tricky. Your brain and body, subject to continual change, find themselves under pressure for decisions supposedly to make or break your life. In contrast with your own feelings and desires, keeping up with school, friends, and societal and parental expectations leaves your mind in torment.

While the typical teen's issues with smoking, bullying, drinking, peer pressure, underage sex, and sleep deprivation are not new, how the modern generation sees and responds to these pressures has changed over time.

Low self-esteem with body image is at an all-time high, particularly in teen girls, as social media feeds growing minds with unending pictures of what is deemed to be perfection. While magazines, movies, music videos, and TV shows used to be the main sources of "celebrity culture," it is now easily accessible with only a few clicks. Cyberbullying and social media use, in general, have increased negative emotional health difficulties.

Teens frequently experience anxiety when confronted with change, and this feeling only intensifies as they approach closer to graduation and start to experience the added pressure of getting accepted to university or selecting a career path. I remember my days. You must also want to leave the nest when you turn 18 and enjoy freedom. Little did I know that this freedom comes with a lot of responsibility, which I was not ready for. It took me about three years to learn the basic skills any teen should know before leaving the house. It was slow and painful because I was running away from adulthood.

But you know what? Being your own boss is so COOL!

Life skills teach you to be independent. Every teen needs a broad range of psycho-social and personal skills known as life skills in order to live a fulfilling and healthy life. These are the abilities that can support your mental health and competence. Teenagers experience various physical, emotional, social, and cognitive changes during the stressful and turbulent time of adolescence. They will help you learn basic domestic skills and financial wellness, maintain your physical and mental health, make logical judgments and much more. Basically, they teach you how to do "life."

Unless you are not living on earth with millions of human beings, you need life skills.

This book is focused on empowering you with the skills you need to keep your mental health in check, maintain your physical health, develop domestic and technical skills, make goals and achieve them, move out, get ready for college, be financially independent, buy and repair your car and everything in between.

You will find 101 skills in the book, divided into eight categories. It will be your light to guide you towards a happier and healthier lifestyle. You would not have to live off, takeouts or wear dirty laundry.

You might be thinking at this point, "Who are you? Why should I listen to you?" I am a life coach with six years of professional experience. I have helped hundreds of overwhelmed teens like you explore the best in themselves and confidently walk into adulthood. All you need is a little nudge towards the right direction, and you will be alright! All the strategies mentioned in the book are result proven for my teen clients to live independently and make the most of this transitioning phase of their life.

Let's not wait anymore. All you need for the best life is in the book!

Here comes the first life skill.

CHAPTER 01

YOU ARE SWISS CHEESE! TOP TIER AND FULL OF HOLES

I am sure you have seen Swiss cheese. What does it look like?

It is full of holes and imperfections, yet it is popular for being one of the healthiest cheeses. We are just like that! Our imperfections and different tastes make us unique, and who we are and our past mistakes do not define our value.

Your Imperfections make you unique.

Most of the time, our stress and anxiety root in the feeling that we do not fit in society's standards or that we are crippled by the guilt of our past mistakes. Unfortunately, this stress and anxiety grow and makes room in your brain.

Here is a story of a teen struggling with a mental health crisis. Most teen girls with body image issues can relate to this.

"It was a day before homecoming. I was eagerly awaiting the end of math lesson, my last period of the day since I was thrilled to be attending the dance with my boyfriend at the moment. When my teacher's phone rang at that point, everything fell apart.

I had a standard checkup with my doctor the previous evening. I left the appointment knowing that my family and doctors were worried about my weight and possibly my mental health. Although, I could not conceal the fact that I had dropped 45 pounds in just three months, I believed—or perhaps I had simply hoped—that I was safe. It was not the case at all.

After that phone call, I was crying and pleading not to be taken to the hospital within two hours. I had the impression that if I were admitted to the hospital, the world as I knew it, would end. How would I spend time with my friends? How would I complete my homework on time? How do I see my family?

I never did any of it anyway.

I hardly saw my friends when my eating disorder was at its worst. I avoided speaking to my family. I withdrew, retreating into my room like a hermit, obsessed with the terrible thoughts that constantly invaded my mind. At school, I lost my normally outgoing and upbeat demeanor; I stopped talking, spent all of my time staring at something on my phone (which turned out to be nonstop videos of food), and changed into someone I could not recognize, not even myself.

I may have claimed to be overjoyed about the weight loss, and perhaps deep down, I did feel that way, but I was so mentally and physically exhausted that I was unable to feel anything other than hunger and tiredness. I struggled so much to get out of bed every morning at my normal time as my health was deteriorating, staying in bed as long as I could before school. I had a hard time staying up in class and watched helplessly as my work ethic declined. I had always given my all to my schoolwork, but at this point, my mind was so occupied that I had no interest in learning or grades."

According to a 2019 Journal of Abnormal Psychology study, teen mental health issues are getting worse. In fact, the present upward trend in teens needing mental health care has been characterized by mental health practitioners as an epidemic.

50% of all lifetime cases of the mental disease start by the age of 14.

So let's learn some skills that would help you improve your mental health.

Navigating the Emotion Compass

The brain enters this phase of rapid development during the teen years. Hormones change, the limbic system is at its peak, and many changes in attitude, maturity, and emotions happen. You need to learn emotional regulation, which refers to the internal process of controlling your emotions, mental state, and behavior in response to internal and external stimuli. Most of us have to learn these skill sets that help us deal with strong emotions, despite the fact that emotional regulation is frequently considered a skill of common sense.

- **How to Understand Your Emotions?**

    Learning to recognize and comprehend your feelings takes work.

    ### Recognize the Emotion

    Pay attention to both your body and your feelings. You can feel physical sensations associated with certain emotions, such as your face getting hot or your muscles tensing up.

Name All Emotions Coming Up

Try to put a name to your unpleasant emotions, such as anger, when they arise. For instance,

- I am really annoyed with Andrew in my study group.
- I become extremely jealous when I see that girl/guy with my ex.
  Every time I have to pass those bullies, I get nervous.

Know the Reason behind Your Feelings

Find out what occurred to cause you to feel the way you do.

For instance, Andrew always manages to find a way to take all the credit whenever we work on group projects.

Although Andrew never contributes his ideas, our teacher views him as the team's leader.

My ex's flirty behavior with other people serves as a reminder that I still have feelings for him or her.

Even though the bullies do not target me, I worry when I watch what they do to other people.

Do not Hide Your Feelings from Yourself

You might not want to make your emotions known to others (like your ex, for instance, or that boy in your study group who is making you mad). However, do not completely repress your emotions. It is much better to acknowledge the emotion than to hide it or to lose control and erupt.

Avoid the Blame Game

It is not the same as assigning blame for how you feel to someone or anything just because you can identify and explain your emotions. The person who steals credit for your effort may not be aware that he is doing it, and your ex is probably not seeing someone new as a strategy to get even with you. You control how you feel when these things occur. Your emotions are there to assist you in making sense of what is happening.

Accept Your Feelings as Normal and Understandable

Do not criticize yourself for your feelings. It is common to experience these. Do not be hard on yourself; acknowledging how you feel can help you move on.

- ## How to Act on Your Emotions?

You can decide whether you need to express your emotion once you have given what you are experiencing some thought. Sometimes simply realizing how you feel is sufficient, but other times you will want to take action to feel better.

Consider Your Options for Expressing Your Feelings

Do you need to calmly confront someone else right now? Discuss your feelings with a friend. Maybe go for a run to get rid of the emotion?

For instance:

"I should not express my anger to Andrew because doing so might make him feel superior. But my gut is telling me to stay away from another situation when he takes leadership of a project."

"I will keep my head held high around my ex. Then I will put on some sad music and have a big cry in my room to help me let go."

"It is a red sign that they have gone too far when I am scared to be near those bullies. Maybe I should discuss my situation with a school counsellor."

Develop Positive Emotions

Happiness and well-being are produced by having positive feelings. Make it a practice to acknowledge and concentrate on the positive aspects of your life, even the tiny ones, like the compliment your father gave you for organizing his bookshelves or how delicious the salad you prepared for lunch is. Even when you are having a difficult day, focusing on the positive aspects of life might help you change your emotional equilibrium from bad to good.

Find Out How to Change Your Mood

You will want to change your attitude from being unhappy to being happy at some point. Otherwise, you risk having a fixed perspective on how awful things are, which will only make you feel worse. Try to do the things that make you happy even if you don't feel like it then. Even if you might not want to leave the house after a breakup, going for a walk or watching a hilarious movie with friends can lift your spirits. You are irritated and frustrated, whether your best friend cancels plans to spend more time with someone else or someone is spreading false information about you online.

It is possible that you feel pressure to perform better than everyone else to protect "your future," This pressure is making you so stressed that you are missing sleep and feeling your weight change.

How can you feel okay when everyone around you seems to be experiencing the thrill and possibilities of teen life except for you? Right?

The above skills will help you deal with this emotional roller coaster.

A Journey to Self-love and Self-Confidence

Each of us is a unique individual. We are aware that this is the case, but let's look at how we are different. Although we are all going through similar events, we all have different perspectives because of who we are as people and where we come from. Even though we share same experiences, our perspective allows for individual manifestations that we refer to as our lives. The mysterious element that gives us the ability to express our uniqueness, talents, and perspectives is our unique consciousness.

When you accept yourself with all your uniqueness, you will feel confident in who you are and start to love yourself. Did you know?

More than 70% of girls aged 15 to 17 skip participating in routine everyday activities like going to school when they feel self-conscious about their appearance. When your body changes, you might feel insecure about it, and it might complicate how you relate it to your sense of self-worth. Moreover, your sexual preferences might also make teen life extra hard. Also, do not be afraid of mistakes. Let's see how we can educate ourselves.

- ## How to Love Yourself?

    ### Avoid Comparisons with Others

    We are taught to be competitive, therefore it comes easily to us to compare ourselves to others. It could, however, be dangerous. Comparing yourself to anyone else on the planet serves no value because there is only one of you. Instead, concentrate on you and your experience. Your sense of freedom will be aided by the energy change alone.

    ### Mistakes are Okay

    We are repeatedly informed as children that "nobody's flawless. Everyone makes errors." But as you age, you feel more pressure to succeed at all costs. Give yourself a break! Make errors so you can learn from them and improve. Accept your past. You are continually evolving from the person you were yesterday into who you are now and who you will be tomorrow.

    So ignore the voice inside your head that tells you to be flawless. Make a lot of mistakes! You will learn invaluable lessons.

Think about Your Fears

Fear is a normal and human emotion, just like making mistakes. Recognize your fears rather than rejecting them. Your mental health will benefit greatly from this beneficial practice. You might get insight and uncover life issues that were causing you to worry by questioning and analyzing your anxieties. That, in turn, may lessen some of your tension, if not all of it.

Seize Any Opportunity that Comes Your Way or Make Your Own

It will never be the perfect time to take your next significant life step. Even though the circumstances may not be ideal, you shouldn't let that stop you from achieving your objectives and aspirations. Instead, take advantage of the time because it might not come again.

Do not Bother What People Think

Do not worry about what people think of you or what they anticipate of you in that same vein. This is a waste of time and will only cause you to go more slowly toward being the best version of yourself because you cannot keep everyone happy.

- ## How to Develop Self-Esteem and Self-Confidence?

    ### Recognize What You Are Good At

    We also have a tendency to love what we are good at, which can lift our moods.

    ### Be More Assertive

    In order to be powerful, one must insist that others respect their wants and ideas. One strategy is to copy aggressive conduct you see in other people.

    The objective is not to pretend to be someone you are not. It entails letting your genuine self shine and taking advice from positive role models.

Reframe Your Self-Judgmental Statements

You can practice positive reframing when you become more aware of your critical thoughts. Reframing a positive concept into a positive or neutral one is positive reframing. This can take the form of statements such as "Wow, I must have sounded like a complete moron asking so many questions in that class," into "I asked many questions. Now I have cleared some of my confusion about the subject," or "My arms are so big" might be translated into "My arms are strong."

Make a List of the Qualities You Value Most about Yourself

It can be challenging or even unpleasant to take a seat and reflect on your many positive traits. However, recognizing your strengths or other elements of yourself might help you improve the way you communicate about yourself. Consider keeping a notebook of your favorite or most admirable actions. Keeping a gratitude notebook is a wonderful way to enhance your view on life and become more aware of your blessings.

Do not just jot down any affirmation that is positive that you come across. Find appropriate affirmations instead, and think about how to accept yourself. What do you value and aspire to be like? When you notice that your mind is filled with negative thoughts, keep in mind these qualities. Keep your mantras personal to you and steer clear of generic ones.

Begin Expressing "No"

People with low self-esteem frequently feel pressured to say yes to requests from others, even when they do not really want to. You run the danger of becoming stressed out, bitter, furious, and depressed.

Go Beyond Your Comfort Zone

- People with low self-esteem typically avoid opportunities and challenges. Perhaps this is the result of fears or self-doubt. But whenever you do something, no matter how small, you show that you can endure in the face of adversity.

How to Deal with Bullying?

Do not interact with verbal bullies; they want you to interact with them, so they have a reason to continue picking on you. Do not interact with the bully if they are not interfering with your daily activities at school or home. If you can, get out of the situation when the bully starts verbally abusing you. Just leave if it is safe for you to do so.

Have a Conversation with the Bully if it is Safe

Numerous unsolved concerns contribute to the behavior of many bullies. Having a talk with the bully may help them understand how much their acts are affecting you and, perhaps, discourage them from continuing, even though this does not excuse their behavior.

Report it

After speaking with them, if the bully still persists, you should report the situation to a higher authority. You can tell a teacher if it is happening at school or your parents if it is happening at home. You should think about calling the police if you believe you are in danger of physical harm from the bully.

Protect Your Personal Space

Draw clearer boundaries and defend your personal space if a family member is making you feel uncomfortable at home. This can entail asking a family member who is currently living with you to leave or, if you have the means, moving out on your own.

Get Help

Seeking assistance to deal with a bully may seem embarrassing, but you should never hold back from doing so. Inform a friend or close family member that you are being bullied.

- ## How to be Sexually Educated?

Sex is complicated. It has SO MANY facets, and there are SO MANY things to think about before, during, and after doing it. Whether you have had sex before or are about to have your first experience, there is a good chance you still have a lot of questions.

How Painful is Your First Time having Sex?

It differs. Some people experience absolutely no pain, while others may find sex to be painful. Some people experience pain when their hymen expands or tears, which might result in little bleeding. It is possible that you would not be aroused enough to have a comfortable encounter (or that you will be feeling scared.)

How to Know When You are really Prepared for Sexual Activity?

Having sex is incredibly private. It can be physical as well as emotional. Teens frequently experience intense sexual feelings, but this does not require them to be acted upon. It is possible to be sexually ready physically but not in the ideal relationship for a variety of reasons. Feeling hurt is simply because having sex can be such a strong emotional experience. Relationships consist of more than just sex.

How to figure out if I am being used Sexually?

In relationships, there are occasions when one partner is ready for sex while the other is not. Since you do not want to compromise what you are not prepared for or what you believe, this might be stressful. You must act in your own best interests. Anyone who tries to coerce you into having sex is not genuinely considering your top priorities.

Is It Preferable to Keep Most of Your Pubic Hair and Trim It rather than Shaving It All Off?

You should do whatever you want with your pubic region! Since they are yours, you must make the final decision. You do not have to keep your pubic hair exactly the same as your friends do, just like you do not dress in precisely the same clothes.

Do I Lose My Virginity If I Have Sex with A Girl?

Virginity is a sensitive subject because of how differently it is treated between men and women. The goal is for guys to lose their virginity. In the meantime, girls are informed that virginity is a gift that they should hang onto, that it is some sort of commodity, and that if they have sex for the first time, they are "losing" something. Virginity is a personal choice that belongs to you and no one else. You can "lose your virginity" in many ways because sex is about close closeness with another person.

- ## How to deal with Body Image Issues?

Identify and Fight Your Negative Thoughts

Who gives a damn what a magazine says about your looks? You are the only one who can assess your value. Pay attention to the self-talk you say to yourself every morning when you look in the mirror. Good or harmful mantras can quickly bloom or fester. Learning about what you have allowed getting ingrained in your inner dialogue is a terrific place to start. Start addressing any unfavorable self-talk you may have as soon as you become aware.

Love Your Body for What It Does for You

Due to an underlying motivation with control being the most prevalent, people frequently criticize or attempt to change their looks. For other people, comfort comes from having control over your look, while so many things are beyond your control. People may become fixated on altering their appearance till it reflects how they want to feel if it does not already. By asking yourself the following questions, you can change your internal narrative. What is your body capable of? On your face, do you feel the wind? Eat some freshly cooked cookies after smelling them in the oven. Whom do you embrace and love?

Show Your Body Love

Everybody's body and every person's needs are unique. Setting up a regimen can help you maintain a healthy physique rather than a thin or fat one. To show your body you care about it, decide what healthy looks like for you and adopt that routine. Get enough rest, consume plenty of water, pursue your passions, and do not forget to appreciate others' efforts as well. Say three beautiful things about yourself for every negative thing you say.

- ## How to Avoid Peer Pressure?

Pay Close Attention to Your Feelings

If anything about a scenario does not feel right, it is probably not right. Even though your friends appear to be fine with the scenario, it might not be the best one for you.

Plan Ahead

Consider your responses to various circumstances. Prepare your speech or action in advance.

Communicate

Tell the person pressing you to stop by talking to him or her and explaining how it makes you feel.

Give a Reason

Saying "no" ought to be acceptable without the requirement for an explanation or an apology. However, suppose you have a solid explanation. In that case, it might be simpler to say no, e.g. claiming that it is harmful to you to take any medication due to a medical condition like allergies or asthma. If you think it would be best to avoid the situation altogether, you may even say that your parents require you to return home.

Make Friends Who Share Your Principles

It is important that you make friends who share your values so you do not get forced into doing anything that does not align with your values.

Get Help

Ask a responsible adult, such as a teacher, parent, or guidance counselor for help. A trustworthy adult is able to listen to you and provide suggestions for possible solutions to your problem. Have you ever noticed that the successful and really popular teenagers at your school are the ones that are not hesitant to express their likes and dislikes? Be fierce and bold!

1.3 Building Meaningful Relationships

How would it feel to get along with everyone at home, in your friendships, and at school even better? Let's break getting along with others down into some specific skills because it sounds rather general and is hard to improve.

- ## How to Make Friends?

Be Genuine

Making friends should not require you to alter who you are; attempting to be someone else all the time is exhausting! Simply be who you are and let others see the genuine you.

A good friend will accept you for who you are; if not, they are not the kind of friend you should be hanging out with.

Remember to maintain an approachable and friendly demeanor at all times by smiling, letting your shoulders down, and fixing your gaze on others rather than covering your face and turning away.

Seek Opportunities to Converse with People

An excellent method to start a discussion with someone is to just say "hi." You might also attempt other ways to start a discussion by complimenting someone. For instance, "I love your jacket. Where did you get that?"

Ask open questions to continue the conversation and learn more about the other person. Open questions are those that allow for responses other than "yes" or "no."

Try New Things with an Open Mind

Meeting new people can occasionally be challenging.

Trying out new interests or activities can help you meet new people because they bring you out and around. This could be participating in community service projects or joining a club at school or elsewhere.

Follow Shared Interests

You can discover that you share similar interests or pastimes after speaking with someone. Doing this can establish a friendship because you already have something in common to talk about or do.

Try to Stay in Touch

A good friendship will be worth the time and effort it takes to develop one.

Maintaining a willingness to communicate will support the friendship. Additionally, you can use this to plan a meeting and do something together or to get to know them better.

- ## How to Avoid Drama and Deal with Fights?

    Let's be real. Reality does not fully prohibit drama. Even for those who make an effort to prevent it, there will inevitably be a little here and there. However, you may take steps to lessen and, in some cases, eliminate it.

    ### End Toxic Relationships

    Saying goodbye to a "friend" who makes you feel horrible does not require an apology. Friends do not try to get in the way of who you are. Instead, they encourage you, give you a place to feel secure, and make you happy.

    ### Avoiding Adding to the Drama

    Trying to fit in with a group might occasionally entail becoming involved in the drama. This might often entail sharing a video you know you should not just because your fake friend told you to or joining the group while they are disparaging someone. When things get out of hand, you can either turn off your phones or remain silent during those controversial chats.

    ### Make a Decision

    You have a choice in how you react to a situation, ALWAYS. You are free to stand by, leave, or stand up.

    ### Fight Constructively

    If you cannot fight a conflict in a useful way, do not fight it at all. You are fighting for the wrong reasons if you aim to inflict harm or simply vent your emotions. You should always try to improve a bad situation in your arguments.

    ### Explain the Issue in Detail

    Try to stick to the facts at first, and then once you have said what the facts are, express your sentiments. To express feelings of rage, hurt, or disappointment, use "I" messages. Avoid using "you" statements like "you irritate me"; instead, use something like "I get irritated when you..."

Invite the Other Person to Express their Viewpoint

Be mindful not to interrupt and make an effort to understand the person's worries and emotions. Try to perceive the situation from the other person's point of view or from his or her point of view. Even if you disagree with the other opinion, you may be able to understand it.

Offer Detailed Solutions, and Encourage the Other Person to Do the Same

Discuss each proposal's benefits and drawbacks.

Be Open to Negotiating

It will be challenging to find a solution if you give the other person only one choice. Celebrate when you decide on a course of action!

How to Approach Someone You Like?

No matter how talkative and confident we may appear to be, we all occasionally find it difficult to talk to individuals we like. So here are some tips for you:

A Smile is Contagious

It actually improves your mood. You will come out as more approachable and less threatening. A beaming smile, in other words, is the boost every conversation needs.

Think Positive

As you approach a stranger, tell yourself encouraging things. Such as, "I look amazing today," "I'm a really confident person," etc.

You will radiate more confidence as a result. It is hot.

Seek Out Similar Ground

Once you feel confident enough to approach them, introduce yourself and look for areas of shared interest. Start by posing a straightforward query; you do not need to be particularly creative. Such as, "Have you been here before?"

Which restaurant is your favorite?

"Do you frequently come here with your friends?"

Are you a person who prefers the outdoors or the indoors?

Inquire about the person's relationship with the host if you are at a party. See if you have any mutual friends. There you go. You have started a discussion.

Make Conversation

Start off by discussing simple subjects like a movie you have seen or a song you like. You can express more of your individuality as soon as the talk starts to flow. Find out if they share your interests by discussing them. Do not limit yourself to self-promotion, though. Ask questions, make eye contact, and show interest by giving several indications that you are listening and genuinely interested.

Flattery will Take You Far

The path to flirting is through flattery. But first, ensure that you feel at ease and that the dialogue moves along. People can detect lies, and doing so would just make you feel uneasy. A compliment should always be given sincerely. Do not bring up private physical characteristics, though. Almost often, it will be offensive. The main safe zones are the eyes, hair, or clothing.

Switch Numbers

Suggest exchanging mobile numbers if the talk goes well and you feel a connection.

Developing social skills will help you prepare yourself for success in the transition to adulthood.

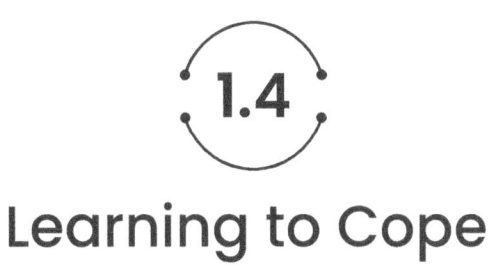

Learning to Cope

I recall the unexpected waves of strong emotion that would wash over me during my own teenage years. Below are positive coping mechanisms for you to relieve your tension and anxiety.

- **How to Meditate?**

    Here are two meditation exercises:

    > **Reverse Counting**

    A smart method to enhance concentration and ease tension in the muscles is reverse or backward counting. With greater focus and devotion, count from 100 to 1 until you reach 1.

    Your stress-related health problems, such as jaw tension, tension headaches, shoulder and neck pain, sleep disturbances and low back pain, are alleviated.

> Deep Breathing

When we are anxious, we frequently breathe quickly and shallowly, raising our heart rates and stress levels.

Close your eyes, sit straight, and take a few calm, deep breaths whenever you are feeling anxious. Following a few seconds of gentle exhalation, listen to or feel your breath from the nose to the bottom. A few slow, deep breaths can instantly relieve stress and help to quiet the mind.

- **How to Problem Solve?**

The quickest approach to relieve stress is frequently to take immediate action to address an issue. This works best when teenagers are dealing with a particular and manageable issue or circumstance rather than general tension and anxiety. Find as much information as you can about the situation, including the people who can help you find a solution. Then break the problem into small parts and address each part separately.

All these skills will help you embrace your unique personality and keep your mental health in check.

Do You Remember?

- What should you consider before acting on your emotions?
- How can you reframe your self-judgmental thoughts?
- Name the first two steps you can take to avoid peer pressure.
- How can you resolve a disagreement with someone?
- What is a problem you have recently faced? What coping technique can you use for it?

CHAPTER 02

LET THAT BODY DO THE TALKING

The human body is a complex and fascinating machine, and so is our world. Did you know?

About 30% of your daily recommended dose of vitamin B6 is found in a banana. Serotonin, which is regarded as a mood stabilizer, is produced in the brain with the aid of vitamin B6. Your emotions and motor abilities are affected by serotonin. It is also a chemical that aids in digestion and sleep. Eating a banana can help with anxiety and depression by increasing serotonin levels.

Let me hook you up with some skills that will help you maintain your physical health. Plus, we all know how your clothes are your reflection. So we will take about that too! This chapter is all about what you put in and on your body.

Taking Care of the Inside

It is critical to look for yourself since everything you do has an impact on your well-being. You should put your attention on activities that are healthy for you and will make you feel your best. You might find that you lack the motivation or energy to do what you love if you do not take care of your well-being. After a few months of leading a healthy lifestyle, you might question why you ever did anything different!

- **How to Choose Healthy Food and Drinks?**

    Controlling your eating habits entails choosing the foods and drinks you consume and the amount you choose. Try to substitute fruits, vegetables, whole grains, low-fat proteins, and fat-free or low-fat dairy products for items that are heavy in sugar, salt, and unhealthy fats.

    Grains

    Instead of refined grain white bread, cereals, and white rice, choose whole grains like brown rice, whole-wheat bread, cereal and oatmeal.

Veggies and Fruits

Make fruits and vegetables the majority of your dish. Vegetables that are red, dark green, or orange are rich in essential nutrients like calcium, vitamin C, and fiber. To include additional vegetables in your lunch, just top your sandwich with spinach and tomato—or any other available greens that you choose.

Dairy

Low-fat or fat-free milk products can help you build strong bones. Choose soy milk or lactose-free milk with additional calcium if you have trouble digesting lactose, a substance found in milk that can give you bloating or gas. Yoghurt, which is low in fat or fat-free, is also a good source of dairy products.

Protein

Lean meats, e.g. turkey or chicken, and other high-protein meals, like egg whites, seafood, beans, tofu and almonds, will give you more energy.

Fats

Your diet must include fat as a necessary ingredient. Fat is necessary for your body to develop and grow, and it may even maintain the quality of your skin and hair. However, lipids provide more calories per gram than protein or carbs, and some of them are dangerous. Some fats are healthier for you than others, such as plant-based oils that are liquid at room temperature. Avocados, seeds, almonds, olives, and seafood such as tuna and salmon fish are examples of foods that contain beneficial oils.

Butter, lard and stick margarine are examples of solid fats that are in solid shape at room temperature. These lipids frequently contain unhealthy saturated and trans fats. Additionally, cheese, fatty meats, and other dairy products prepared from whole milk are foods that include saturated fats. Eat less of the items that are commonly high in trans and saturated fats, such as cheeseburgers, fried chicken, and fries. Consider a turkey, lean-meat or veggie burger, or a turkey sandwich with mustard. Lastly, a limited amount of sodium, which is primarily included in salt, is required by your body.

However, consuming too much sodium in your food and beverages can cause your blood pressure to increase, which is bad for both your heart and the rest of your body. Try to eat no more than 1 teaspoon or 2,300 mg, of sodium per day.

- ## How to have the Best Sleep?

According to studies, teens typically get 8.5 hours of sleep every night, but according to science, they would function better with 10 hours. Lack of sleep can lead to irritation, inability to pay attention, mood swings, difficulty concentrating, learning, listening, and problem-solving.

Avoid Coffee Right before Bed

Coffee, tea, energy drinks, and other beverages contain caffeine. It might keep you awake and aware because it is a stimulant. You might want it first thing in the morning. However, it may cause you to toss and turn in bed at night. Limit your caffeine intake during the day to aid in sleep, and switch to caffeine-free beverages and decaf at night.

Be Active in the Day

You have probably observed how active little children are and how peacefully they sleep. Get at least 60 minutes of exercise each day by learning from a child. Your mood and stress levels can both be improved by physical activity. Just keep in mind that exercising too close to nighttime can wake you up before it slows you down.

Put Away Your Electronic Devices

Establish a tech-free zone in your bedroom. Turning off all electronics 60 minutes before going to bed prevents the brain from believing it is still daylight. Furthermore, you would not be awakened by late-night texts if you turn off your phone.

Maintain a Sleep Schedule

The body learns to anticipate sleep by going to bed at the same time daily. This calming impact can be strengthened by establishing a regular nighttime routine. So every night, unwind by reading, listening to music, playing with a pet, keeping a journal, meditating, or engaging in any other activity that makes you feel at ease.

- ## How to Read the Nutrition Food Label?

Each food and beverage product's main or top portion of the sample nutrition label can contain information specific to that item (calories and nutrient information). A footnote in the bottom section provides information on the % Daily Value and the number of calories used for basic nutritional guidance. See the picture for more description.

To make it easier for you to concentrate, I have highlighted some elements of the following nutrition facts label. Please take note that the real food labels of the products you buy do not contain these colored sections.

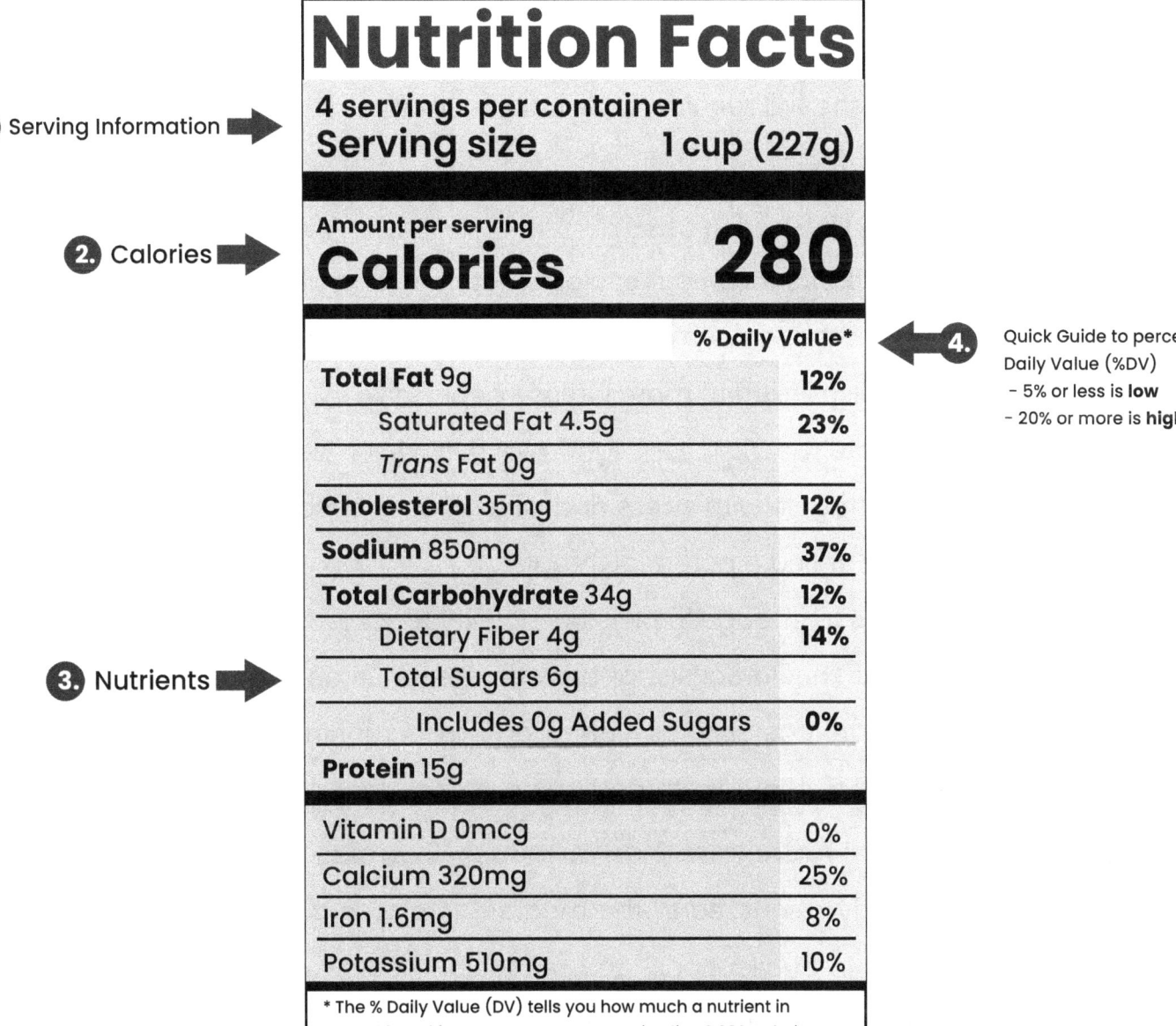

- ## How to Choose Your Food Portion?

  The quantity of food or liquid you choose to consume all at once, whether you are dining out, eating something at school, a friend's house, or your own home, is referred to as a portion. Many people overeat, especially while they're away from home. When you consume meals that are ready to eat from a grocery store, restaurant, or school, you can consume more calories than your body needs to keep you energized. The portion size listed on a food label could be higher or lower than the recommended serving size. That is because your age, current weight and height, metabolism, and level of activity all play a role in how many calories you need daily to stay the same weight or lose weight.

  For example, if a girl's weight is 125 pounds and her primary form of exercise is a quick stroll once a week, she will require fewer calories than a girl of similar size who runs several times each week.

- ## How to Get Enough Exercise?

  Exercise has positive effects on our social, emotional, and physical health, including lower disease risk, better focus, more self-assurance, and less hostility.

  Lack of exercise is also linked to more intense depressive symptoms.

  Exercise can simulate the "fight" or "flight" reaction, which helps signal your brain to calm down if you struggle with stress or anxiety. This is because your mind believes you have fought off or fled a potential threat!

  Experts advise teens to engage in physical activity for at least 60 minutes each day. The majority of that should consist of brisk to strenuous aerobic exercise. Anything that makes your heart race, such as riding, dancing, or running, is considered aerobic. After that, spend a few minutes strengthening your muscles.

  ### Consider Physical Activity rather than just "Exercise

  Exercise is frequently discussed in the media. Exercise is a topic that is frequently highlighted on T.V., in publications, and on social media, whether it be for getting ripped by following a celebrity's workout regimen or seeing advertisements for new active wear brands.

However, physical exercise does not always have to be regimented. Technically, any structured program where certain activities are scheduled and repeated over time is "exercise" (think push-ups, bench presses, doing dance drills, running 3K.) But there are other ways to get your body moving than this kind of structured exercise. You can move your body in a variety of diverse ways.

It is quite acceptable if the idea of getting into athletic attire and going to the gym does not appeal to you. There are many other ways to exercise, including dancing to your favorite music, throwing a Frisbee, playing an active board game or video game, using the stairs rather than an escalator or elevator, or going on a bushwalk with friends or going rock climbing,

Include Exercise in Your Regular Routine

If you enjoy team sports or organized fitness, getting active is probably already a part of your weekly training sessions or lessons calendar. It is time to consider ways you can get active that fit in around your regular schedule, though, if you have realized that being active is not a daily habit.

Try riding your bike or walking to school or work, setting up a lunchtime handball match with friends, or bringing your dog for a stroll every day.

- ## How to Take Care of Your Skin?

If acne outbreaks and pimples have come knocking at your door, it is hardly surprising. But you should not be concerned. Even though 90% of teenagers have acne, it is quickly treatable due to the resilient nature of teen skin.

Cleanse Thoroughly

A foamy or gel cleanser for everyday skincare will usually work well if your skin is oily. Cleanse your skin once daily or twice if it becomes particularly oily or unclean during the day. Buy tissues to blot your face. Try a milky cleanser and moisturizer if you have dry skin as opposed to oily skin.

Control Oil

You need to control the shine without harming your skin. The basic three-step procedure for oil control is as follows: Choose a salicylic acid cleanser, reduce shine with an oil-free primer, and blot oil throughout the day with specialized cloths or tissues.

Purchase the Right Acne Products

If you have an acne break out, try the following method: Apply a toner after cleansing your skin, followed by a medicated acne gel.

Before Going to Bed, Wash Your Face

If you frequently sleep with makeup on, you may experience an acne flare-up or an itchy rash known as periocular dermatitis.

Exfoliate

Only once or twice a week, using a product that is relatively light, is required for exfoliation. Avoid scrubbing (it would not help with blackheads or acne) and excessive exfoliation.

Put on Sunblock

Utilizing sunscreen also prevents the darkening of your acne blemishes. Choose an oil-free product, and search for cosmetics that incorporate sunscreen, such as liquid foundation.

- ## How to Take Care of Your Hair?

    Teenagers often do not take proper care of their hair. Your hair may break or grow more slowly if you ignore it. Hair care might be difficult, especially if you do not have much time, but maintaining healthy, fashionable hair can make you feel more appealing and confident.

    ### Understand Your Hair Type

    Each person has unique hair, frequently requiring a unique treatment and maintenance approach. To build the greatest hair care routine possible, find out your hair type. Observe your hair inclinations by going a few days without using any cosmetics and your natural hair.

If You Need to, Wash Your Hair

Many people think they must wash their hair every day. However, the majority of hair types only require washing every other day or a few times per week. Wash your hair when it is dirty, not merely out of habit, depending on your hair type. In general, thin, straight hair requires more frequent washing than thick, curly or wavy hair.

When Your Hair Is Wet, Comb It

Brushing your hair right after the shower can be tempting because it is a quick way to remove tangles. However, a wide-tooth comb is the most effective tool for removing any knots after showering.

Do a Regular Trim

Split ends are common in hair, and if you go a long time without cutting your hair, it may start to look damaged and unhealthy. Try to trim your hair every three months or every six weeks if you are prone to split ends.

How to Stay Hygienic?

Throughout puberty, your body goes through a number of changes. Your skin and hair may suddenly and easily start to feel oily. It seems as though new hair is growing on you every day in various places. What can you then do?

Shower Daily

Eccrine and apocrine sweat glands are two different types that your body contains. When you exercise yourself, your eccrine glands produce perspiration to control your body temperature. These glands provide an explanation for why you perspire more during soccer practice but not when going to and from class.

During puberty, your apocrine glands release some proteins and you end up smelling like week-old socks when the protein in your apocrine secretions combines with germs on your skin.

Take Caution When Using Tampons

Many teenagers like tampons over pads because they are more hygienic and less likely to ruin pants. Tampons can cause toxic shock syndrome (TSS), a potentially fatal illness if they are left in for too long.

Choosing a menstrual cup does not lessen the risk. Your risk of TSS is increased by any object left in the vagina for an extended period of time. If you find that days with high flow require you to change your pad every two hours, think about investing in period panties for additional leak protection.

Replace Pads Regularly

Even if your flow is modest, you run the danger of odor and infection if you keep your menstrual pad in place all day. Change your pads at least once every six hours for best protection and more frequently if you have a heavy flow.

Utilize Organic Deodorants

You sweat more during adolescence, and it smells riper. Purchase a high-quality deodorant, but use caution when using antiperspirants. While they temporarily block pores to lessen perspiration, they have the potential to affect hormones in humans. Use a natural crystal deodorant instead. This product is free of dangerous chemicals, albeit it takes time to build up and may briefly make you smell bad.

These skills will help you nurture your body and feel great!

2.2

Taking Care of the Outside

The apex of self-expression is fashion.

At first, trying to dress effectively might be stressful and perplexing. However, remember that looking and feeling your best is a goal you can achieve. You can get better at dressing stylishly with some effort and time.

As you move through your closet, clothes fly in all directions. Ugh! You have nothing at all to wear! The following skills will help you develop not any

fashionable but also a practical wardrobe according to your style.

- How to Pick Under Clothes?

   Underwear

   Ten to twenty pairs of underwear are a good number. Include everyday boy shorts or briefs, a couple of seamless pairs, and one or two pairs that are more attractive.

Camisoles

Any teen girl's wardrobe should include a variety of camis. They are excellent for layering and are available at practically all apparel stores. Prioritize neutral hues like white, black, grey, and neutral. You can return for colors once your wardrobe is complete.

Bras

One or more sports bras if you engage in physical activity, two to four neutral, white, black, or pastel-colored everyday bras, one strapless bra, and one or two push-up bras. Darker colors should be avoided because tops can see through them.

Socks

Approximately ten pairs of daily ankle socks, a few pairs of trainer liners, and a few pairs of knee-high or over-the-knee socks should be kept on hand. You could also want a pair of soft or cozy socks.

Tank Tops

Have a few tank tops that are either snug or loose; a fantastic brand is sugar lips.

- ## How to Pick Bottoms?

Have a selection of trendy and functional bottoms. For the summer, you can have a floral skirt or whatever style. Shorts with a high or low rise are both fantastic. Your wardrobe will benefit greatly from adding two pairs of embellished jeans and a pair of dark-wash skinny jeans (with a few pairs). Try bell-bottom jeans for a distinctive pair of jeans. Remember to wear leggings! Look for stylish sweatpants in addition to the standard, baggy variety.

Two to three pairs of sweatpants are ideal. Ensure they are of high quality, a proper fit (not too loose or tight), and at least two of your outfits match.

Try to purchase largely dark or medium-washed jeans because they are the most versatile, but if you fall in love with a pair, do not be hesitant to purchase them.

- ## How to Pick Tops?

    Purchase some fashionable, high-quality clothes that fit you. In general, any tops that match your fashion sense will work. Avoid wearing loose-fitting t-shirts. Sweaters and flowing tops go well together. Do not get into the habit of buying the same shirt in every hue because you enjoy it that much; instead, obtain a range of colors and styles. The ideal range would be ten to fifteen. There is a wide selection at Aeropostale.

    Get one to three everyday coats, one light coat, one or two ski jackets, and one vest if you are in the North or Midwest. One light coat, one heavy jacket and (optionally) one vest should be plenty if you live in the west or south.

    Get a range of tops. Consider stocking your closet with three to four tunics or smart shirts, five to six graphic tees or everyday tops, three long-sleeve tees, three camis, two lounging tees, three cardigans, and four hoodies, for instance (zip-ups too).

- ## How to Pick Dresses?

    Purchase some beautiful dresses for various events. Possess between two and six different clothes, including one black dress and roughly five other dresses. Tall girls look beautiful in long dresses. Try to purchase them in various designs and colors that go well with you. Some should be more formal, like churches, while others should be for parties.

    Have a specific number of dresses. Have one or two formal, four to five casual events and three semi-formal dresses.

- ## How to Pick Shoes?

    Get a range of adorable, reasonably priced, and high-quality shoes. With shoes, you could either hit it or miss it. Do not overuse your credit card, and make sure your shoes are stylish and fit your personality. Listed below are a few pairs to get you going:

Athletic Shoes

Having at least one pair of athletic shoes is recommended. You need at least one pair of running shoes, yet how many sports you participate in will also influence this.

Sneakers

At least one pair of casual sneakers, such as Converse, Vans, or Nike blazers, are required. These are excellent for the mall, a park, or a friend's house.

Sandals

Have a pair or two of adorable, cozy sandals on hand for walking and going to the beach. Also fantastic are moccasins.

Boots

Depending on where you reside, you should have at least one pair of hiking boots. You should also have a pair of long black boots for cold or warm weather. No flashy colors, but black is good. Uggs are incredibly well-liked.

Flats

You should have several pairs of flats because they go in many different outfits. Bright colors or feminine designs always make an ensemble full and transform your appearance. Always have a backup, and perhaps keep a pair of standard black or grey shoes.

Heels

Have one or possibly two pairs of heels. One should unquestionably be in black and perhaps a few more in fashionable hues, but make sure they coordinate with your outfits and formal attire.

- ## How to Dress Smartly?

  Do not overcomplicate things if you want to look stylish as a teenager right away. You can keep your ensembles simple by choosing the appropriate blend of easy-to-wear items that work well together.

Put simplicity first while expanding your collection and purchasing new clothing. To improve your overall sense of style, take out the excess. By maintaining a minimal wardrobe, you can simply improve the way you look.

Simple designs and clothing do not have to be uninteresting. By simply making the most of your closet and choosing the right group of complementary outfits, you can turn every item you own into a winner.

- ## How to Dress for a Job Interview?

When you arrive at the interview dressed professionally, you may make a good impression on the hiring manager and demonstrate how well you would fit in with their workplace. Here is what you can pick from:

Shirt with Buttons and Dark Pants

A button-down shirt and black pants are common clothing choices for many corporate environments. You can choose from a number of colors for your shirt depending on the company and your particular taste. Consider neutral colors like white or black if the business is more formal or traditional. Depending on your unique taste, you could use boots or formal shoes with this ensemble.

A Polo and Khakis or Pants

Another excellent option is a polo paired with dress slacks or khakis, depending on the season. You might wear this attire if you are interviewed for a summer job or a position in a warm location. Polo shirts can be worn in a number of colors, but it is recommended to go with muted hues to reduce distractions. You might also wear something straightforward like stripes. Consider wearing a belt and tucking your shirt into your slacks to preserve a professional image. Dress shoes or loafers are acceptable shoe choices.

Mid-Length Dress

Another common option is a dress, which comes in a wide range of different style possibilities. Dresses for business occasions should be mid-length or roughly knee-length. You might wear a dress with tights, a sweater, or a blazer, depending on the time of year. You can choose flats, low-heeled wedges, or loafers as footwear.

Wear a Blouse or Dress Shirt with a Skirt or Pants

You can also pair slacks or a skirt with a blouse or dress shirt. Choose a blouse with a soothing color or a straightforward design, like stripes. Choose khakis or slacks for your pants. In order to wear a blouse with a skirt, choose one that is mid-thigh in length or just above the knee. Dress shoes or a simple pair of flats can be used to complete this look.

- ## How to Shop Wisely?

Visit the Clearance Racks to Shop

When you walk into a store, even if there are other items that capture your eye, go straight for the sale rack. Particularly at the pricey stores, they provide the best discounts.

Visit Discount Stores

That includes secondhand shops! Some bargain retailers sell name brands that the store does not want. Discount retailers include establishments like Burlington and T.J. Maxx. Everything is new, and it has never been worn. What is best? Even on the price tag, it says how much you save!

Look for Sales

Even though you are on a tight budget, you can still treat yourself to a few stylish new items. You have to take advantage of sales in order to save money, especially if you want to purchase items from an expensive retailer. The simplest method to achieve this is to sign up for a lot of catalogues and advertisements. It also keeps you abreast of the most recent fashions and trends.

Here's to feeling and looking great!

Do You Remember?

- What are the examples of whole grains?
- How many minutes before sleeping should you put away your phone?
- What does the daily percentage value represent on the food nutrition labels?
- What kind of cleanser will work for your skin if it is oily?
- How frequently do you need a trim?
- After how long should you change pads?
- How many underwear do you need?
- Where can you go if you want to shop economically?
- What can you pair with a skirt for a job interview?

CHAPTER 03

NOTHING HOTTER THAN BEING SELF-SUFFICIENT

Why is being self-sufficient one of the most crucial success factors? Because they can only help you get where you want to go, your family, friends, and loved ones cannot take you there. You are already in control of the travel planning process. When others let you down or fail you, all you have is yourself.

People who wish to have greater control over their lives and believe they do not need others to achieve their aims must develop their independence. Being more independent will allow you to do as you like without worrying about what other people think, and it will also inspire you to come up with novel solutions to your difficulties. As you gain independence and control your own destiny, you might experience relief and joy.

The skills added in this chapter will help you be independent and achieve your freedom goals.

Domestic Skills

Domestic skills are ones that you use at home and are frequently needed in day-to-day activities. Everyone needs these fundamental abilities to maintain tidy and healthy living spaces. Let's get started.

- ## How to Shop for Groceries? Make a List of Items You Need

    First of all, it is crucial to make a grocery list. Whenever I went to grocery shop list without writing everything down I came home with at least five unnecessary items.

    ### Establish a Spending Limit.

    Surprisingly, blowing through your budget at the grocery shop is simple. Making a budget also stops you from buying unnecessary amounts of junk food.

    Keep as near to the store's edge as possible.

    When doing your food shopping, it is really simple to become lost in the supermarket. Therefore, I go outside the store first when I am trying to enter and exit the store without purchasing a lot of junk food. Typically, the necessities can be found there, and it is simpler to see what is on each aisle without going there.

    ### You Need a Shoppers Card

    They are frequently free and useful for exclusive member promotions. The money you save can make up for the occasional annoyance of receiving emails from a food store.

    The best products are not usually those with a known brand.

    We are all prone to label obsession at times, but branded goods are not always superior to store brands. Since many generic brands taste the same and are less expensive, you will have more money to use to dine out.

    ### Browse the Frozen Food Section Last

    Nothing is worse than purchasing ice cream at the start of a grocery shop visit and melting it before you even reach the register. By going to the frozen food section last, you can avoid having to make two journeys there.

- ## How to Cook Simple Meals?

The sooner people can learn to prepare their own meals and discover what is and is not healthy for them, the better. We all like having our parents prepare our meals when we are young. However, when you enter your teen years, it is a good idea to try to educate yourself on how to succeed and make wise decisions in the kitchen.

Read the Recipe before Anything Else

You must read the complete recipe before beginning to prepare food. I have done this before. I started making a dish I wanted to be finished in an hour before discovering the meat needed to be marinated for at least 2 hours! This seems obvious, like many of our cooking tips and methods... nonetheless, we have all been in this situation! The following tips will help you be efficient in making meals.

Learn Which Vegetables Freeze Best and How to Prolong the Life of Items.

Some veggies are excellent for freezing, while others are perfect for pickling or canning.

What freezes easily: blanched green beans, Root vegetables, blanched carrots, frozen spinach balls (Roasted or Mashed) and sautéed spinach. Both mashed avocado and banana freeze well, although they still oxidize when exposed to air.

Keeping Food Fresher for Longer: The finest containers are always airtight ones. For advice, push down with plastic wrap or toss your vegetables with a little olive oil to help prevent freezer burn.

Make use of Mise en Place

"Mise en place" is to prepare everything in advance! I can remember times when I had to stop cooking to mince garlic or cut an onion. And I often pondered why it took me 2 hours to prepare a "20-minute" meal. Simple on the surface, but much too frequently ignored because cooking may be started straight away.

- **How to Do Laundry?**

You will need to do your laundry sooner or later. The following steps will help you wash your clothes.

- Divide the light and the dark. Keep in mind that these need to be washed separately. The next time you are at the grocery store, pick up some color catchers. They are offered in the same aisle as the laundry soap, preventing color bleed.
- Pre-treat stains and check pockets.
- Check the washing instructions label on the clothes for delicates and dry cleaning only.
- Pour in the detergent.
- Set the water's temperature as desired. Use warm or hot water for the lights. Use chilly water for darks.
- Start the machine, then add the clothing. Set a timer on your watch or phone to remind you to check the washer in about 45 minutes.
- Move the load into the dryer once the cycle is finished.
- For efficiency and safety (to avoid fires), clean the dryer vent.
- Add dryer balls or dryer sheets (optional.)
- Select the time and settings, then turn on the dryer. Once more, set a timer to help you remember to return.

- **How to Tidy Up Your Room?**

Cleaning your room could seem like a tedious chore, or it might be so disorganized that you do not even know where to begin. Even while it may not be enjoyable, consistently cleaning your room will keep it less crowded and help you feel more at home there. Before you begin cleaning your shelves, floors, and tables, start by selecting enjoyable music and setting timers to make the process feel more enjoyable.

Clean and Make Your Bed

Clear your bed of anything other than the sheets, blankets, and pillows (put them away). Make the bed next. The following few steps should not be hampered by disorganized sheets.

Collect Your Clothes on the Bed and Place them where They Belong

Now search your room and the rest of the home for all the garments. Put it right in the hamper if something is dirty. After that, fold (or hang) the clean clothing and store it.

Take Everything that is not needed in the Room and Dispose of the Garbage

Pick up anything that is still on the floor and try to find a place for it.

Suppose the air in your room has a strange odor. Sprinkle some vinegar over the carpet or rug. Just let it sit here for a while.

Get Furniture Surfaces Clean (Dresser, Nightstand, Bookshelves, Desk)

Take a quick, pleasant-smelling cleanser in your hand, and clean the dust off. If you cannot find a Swiffer or cleaner, even a damp paper towel is preferable to nothing. Remember the fan too.

Vacuum the vinegar off the rug or carpet. If you have hardwood floors, clean them with a Swiffer or broom.

- ## How to Hang a Picture?

    You should measure the area and test your layout on the floor before hanging anything, starting with your largest or most prominent element. You will need the following:

    - Measuring tape
    - Stud finder
    - Pencil
    - 4 ft. level
    - Brackets/hooks/wire mounts

- Nails/screws
- Check your placement prior to making any holes. Anything weighing more than 50 pounds requires a stud. Suppose you can relate to this. Locate a stud using the stud finder, and then modify your layout accordingly.
- Mark and measure. As you adjust your measurements, using sticky notes for an approximate placement can be incredibly beneficial. The approximate center and top of where you wish to hang your pieces should be marked with a sticky note.
- Measure the distance from the top of your painting to the ceiling. Next, measure the placement of the hanger on the back of the photo. For instance, if you are hanging something 10 inches from the ceiling and the hanger is 3 inches from the top of the piece, the nail or screw should be positioned at 13 inches from the ceiling to ensure optimum hanging height.
- If you have an item that needs a hanger on each side, level it. Before installing the second hanger, level the piece with a level positioned on top of the piece after measuring for one side.

- ## How to Clear a Clogged Sink?

  The clogs that can build in bathroom sinks due to toothpaste, soap scum, hair, and other hygiene products can be difficult to clear. However, several less-expensive alternative techniques for unclogging are quite simple and easy to use before you call a plumber.

  ### Use Vinegar with Baking Soda

  This is a tried-and-true method for unclogging drains that work wonders in bathroom sinks. Just combine 1/3 cup of baking soda with the same amount of vinegar and in a measuring cup.

  This mixture will bubble right away, so you should quickly dump it down the drain. The hair and dirt are effectively removed thanks to the fizzing action. After letting it stand for about an hour, add hot water.

- ## How to Unclog a Toilet?

    Plunge the toilet bowl using the plunger. Make sure the plunger covers the hole entirely. Fully submerge the plunger in the water so that only water, not air, may be forced or pulled through the aperture.

    If there is not much water in the bowl to completely submerge the plunger, add some water from the bathroom sink.

    Pump the plunger over the hole. As the first plunge will force air into the bowl, begin slowly at first. To upset and loosen the blockage, push down and quickly pull up. Once the water starts to drain, keep pulling and pushing firmly. Before the toilet clears, it can take 15 to 20 cycles.

    Be tolerant. Plunging alone frequently works as long as no hard item is lodged inside. Although it might not work right away, it frequently does after a few dozen plunge cycles.

    To inspect the drainage, flush the toilet. Keep the plunger in the bowl and re-fill it with water if it ultimately drains, but the obstruction still prevents a free flow down the drain. Fill it to the level it would be after a typical flush, then plunge. You might have to repeat this process numerous times to clear stubborn clogs.

    Once you have finished plunging, flush the toilet 2-4 times to let the obstruction go through the sewer system.

- ## How to Deal with a Fire at Home?

    Your life may be saved if you know what to do in a fire.

    ### If You Can, Put Out the Fire

    You might be able to put out a fire that had just started, such as one that started when a skillet caught fire on the stove.

    Grab your fire extinguisher and use the PASS method to put out the fire: pull the pin, aim it at the flames' base, squeeze the handle, and move the extinguisher from side to side. Verify that the fire has completely been put out and is not still spreading.

To Escape, Scurry beneath the Flames

When a structure is on fire, smoke and hazardous gases are produced, which can make it difficult to escape because they can make you dizzy or cause you to lose consciousness if you breathe them in. Crawl to the nearest exit, keeping in mind that it might be a window to escape the fire and its gases. Keeping a low profile will assist in shielding you from breathing in smoke and dangerous substances.

Check the Doors and Doorknobs for Heat

Check to see if the door is hot and if you have to pass through it to reach an exit. Do not enter if the door (or doorknob) feels warm to the touch since a fire may be burning on the other side. Shut the door and proceed to a second exit if you open a door and observe fire or smoke.

Run for Cover

When you reach the outdoors, quickly flee the fire to safety. Run down the block or across the street for safety, as a portion of the home or apartment, such as the roof or siding, could catch fire and fall around the building's perimeter.

Now let's move on to some skills that will help you be independent outside of your house.

Technical Skills

Teen independence is wonderful because it allows you to make more of your own decisions, choose who you want to be, and develop self-reliance. The practical skills mentioned in this chapter are more technical and will help you move a step up your independence ladder.

- **How to Schedule a Doctor's Appointments?**

  Throughout your teenage years, you must schedule regular visits with a primary care physician. You are growing and developing at a crucial point in your life. You might wish to talk with your doctor about a few issues as your body changes.

  > You should not worry about bringing copies of your medical records when making an appointment with a doctor you have been seeing for a while. You will already have everything there for you. Your medical records should be transferred in advance of your appointment if you're going somewhere new. Your health insurance card should be with you as well. Bring extra cash to cover the co-pay if your insurance requires one for your appointment.

  > There are many factors to consider while looking for a doctor you can trust. It is crucial that you feel at ease speaking with your doctor. Any situation in your life that might be harming your health should be disclosed to him or her. Consider the various characteristics you want in a primary care physician if you need to choose a new physician. You can get referrals from friends and relatives. Examining online reviews for doctors or clinics can also be helpful.

  > You must be completely honest with yourself regarding your health and well-being. Inform your doctor of your symptoms if you are going through anything that you believe might be alarming. It could be time to choose a new doctor if you feel awkward discussing your symptoms with your current one. The time during your doctor's appointment is the ideal opportunity to ask any questions you may have regarding your body or health. Make sure you receive the explanation you need.

- ## How to Take the Bus?

   While learning how to use a bus to travel from point A to point B may seem difficult, it is typically quite straightforward. You will be able to ride the bus like an expert after a few rides.

   ### Look at a Bus Route Map

   Almost all public transportation buses follow a predetermined route. Get a bus route map to learn how to get where you need to go. These often contain lines of various colors with dots representing the various buses and stations along them. A timetable showing the locations of each bus's scheduled stops should be included on the bus route map.

   These bus route maps are often available online at the city's transportation website or at nearby establishments like stores, restaurants, and schools that are close to bus lines.

   As the city you are in can have alternative timetables or routes these days, look for a separate route map for weekends and holidays.

   ### For Arrival and Departure Times, See the Timetable on the Route Map

   While each bus route map is unique, they typically all include a timetable. The bus arrival and departure times for each stop along a specific route should be shown on the timetable. Write down the arrival time for the stop that is closest to you and locate the portion of the schedule that details your route.

   Bus schedules frequently have color coding to indicate each route.

   Look for a piece of the schedule that is highlighted in yellow.

   ### If Your City Provides an Online Trip Planner, Use It

   Visit the webpage for public transit in your city online. Look for a trip planner for public transportation that enables you to enter your starting point, destination, and perhaps even the time of day you wish to go. Once you enter this information, the feature will probably provide the best course of action.

Purchase a Bus Pass or Use Money to Cover the Fare

If you wish to take the bus, you must pay a fare. Most regular bus users purchase a pass, which they use for convenience and efficiency. A bus pass can typically be purchased via the city's public transportation office or website.

- ## How to Defend Yourself?

It is critical to realize that self-defense does not equate to "fighting skills." In reality, self-defense entails taking all reasonable precautions to avoid engaging someone who threatens, intimidates, or attacks you. It involves employing your brains, your instincts, and your wits.

Run

In the event that you are ever being pursued or attacked by someone, this is perhaps the best option you could think of. Your initial thought will probably be to flee and ask someone for assistance. As a result, whenever you manage to escape an attacker's grasp, run as rapidly as your legs will allow you to.

Make Use of Your Bows

It would not be a great idea to punch the attacker. We advise using your forearms and elbows in place of doing that. Take hold of the attacker's neck with one hand, slash his eyes, and then elbow him in the face.

Always Choose Eyes First

An assaulter is knocked off balance when he is initially struck in the eye. Not only would it injure him, but it would also leave him open to attack. Therefore, always aim for his eyes first anytime you sense an assailant is trying to attack you. Scratch their eyeballs with your thumbs.

Try Out Bicycle Kick

Never forget to employ the bicycle kick if the attacker tries to attack you and knocks you to the ground. Utilize your legs to repeatedly kick the attacker in the face until he falls off.

Attack the Groin

Attacks on the attacker's groin always hurt, especially if the attacker is a man. You can grab hold of his neck or shoulders with your hands before kicking him in the groin with your knee. The attacker will groan in agony and take a step back as a result. You can leave the situation in the meantime.

- ## How to Use First AID?

Regardless of age, learning fundamental first aid skills is crucial.

Get Ready

Make sure you have some necessities in your room. These include gauze, bandages, an electronic thermometer, cold and flu medicines, lozenges, and antibiotic cream.

> - To treat minor burns, place the affected area under three to five minutes of cool (not cold) running water before covering it loosely with gauze. Avoid applying ice or cream to the burn.
>   Whenever a blister appears, do not pop it.
>   For pain relief, take Advil, Motrin, or Tylenol.
> - Press a bandage or clean cloth on the wound for stopping the bleeding for minor cuts or scratches. After washing the wound with water, use an antibiotic cream e.g. Neosporin to treat it. Apply a bandage. Be sure to replace it whenever it gets dirty or damp.
> - If you have a fever, make sure to drink plenty of water and hydrate your body with warm water.
> - Use over-the-counter cold medications to treat coughing. Suck lozenges (pills for sore throat), have some honey, and drink tea.

If someone is seriously injured:

- Call your country's emergency helpline and request an ambulance.
- Treat any obvious wounds.
- If the person can be laid down due to their injuries, do so with their legs raised and supported if possible.
- Put a blanket or coat on them to keep them warm.
- Do not offer them drinks or food.
- Offer them a lot of comfort and assurance.
- Keep an eye on the injured person; if they stop breathing, begin CPR and notify the emergency services once more.

- ## How to Communicate Well?

Many of us engage in everyday social interaction with others, whether in person or via the numerous digital channels at our disposal. How much of our communication, though, actually has the desired impact on the intended audience? If we wish to communicate effectively, we must be thorough and exact.

Effective communication is the process of exchanging thoughts, concepts, information, and facts to make sure that the message is received and understood clearly and with a purpose. When we communicate well, both the sender and the recipient are happy.

Being clear, complete, correct, compassionate and concise are all characteristics of effective communication. You may not agree with our definition of the "5 C's of communication," though. Like any other talent, communication is one that you can get better at with practice. Here are some tips to start enhancing your communication abilities.

- **Consider Your Listener**

    Consider your audience carefully because the people you want to reach might not be the same as the people you really do. If you want to deliver the right messaging in an effective manner, knowing your audience is essential. Age, race, gender, ethnicity, income, marital status, subject knowledge, education level, and professional experience are just a few of the variables that can affect how others receive your message.

- **Clarify Your Point as Much as You Can**

    You might have something to say once you have effectively identified your audience and listened to their goals, wants, and desires.

- **Use Active Listening Techniques**

    Active listening involves giving a dialogue exchange your full attention. A few tactics include paying attention to body language, posing inquiries, offering encouraging verbal cues, and acting in a nonjudgmental manner. Consider your audience before you talk, and pay attention to what they really want and need.

- **Respect the Views and Feelings of the Other Person**

    Treating people with respect in your interactions with them lets them know that you cherish your relationship with them and can help even tense situations go more smoothly.

- **Learn the Art of Compromising**

    This does not imply that you must compromise or repress your beliefs. Try to talk about options that will benefit both of you. Everyone may be able to move forward and feel good about it by reaching a compromise.

Do You Remember?

- How can you get a shopper's card?
- What is Mise en Place?
- What kind of water temperature you need to use for washing light and darkclothes?
- What can you use to get rid of the funky smell in your room?
- How many cycles do you need to unclog your toilet?
- Do you need your medical records when going to a doctor?
- How can you get a bus pass?
- How can you treat small burns?

These skills will be valuable in your adult life and maximize your teen life potential.

EYES ON THE PRIZE CHAMP!

Our brains carry out many functions that are required for thinking, acting, and problem-solving. They are collectively referred to by psychologists as executive functioning. Executive functioning will help you achieve your personal and professional goals.

Our ability to learn new information, retain that information in our minds, and use it to solve issues in daily life all fall under the category of executive functioning.

A person can live, work, and learn with adequate competence and independence for their age, thanks to their executive functioning skills. People can obtain information, consider options, and implement those solutions thanks to executive functioning.

A group of mental abilities known as executive function include self-control, planning, working memory, and flexibility of thought. Executive functioning issues prevent some people from performing these tasks naturally.

Let's include some skills in executive functioning.

How to Set Goals?

You need to have a dream before you can create a goal. Something you consider a dream. You strive to achieve it. It is a potential result. A dream is, therefore, a vision of who you want to become and where you want to go in the future. Dreams can, therefore, only be realized, not accomplished.

Another difference between objectives and dreams relates to outcomes. A dream has no outcomes since it is a glimpse of the future. Dreaming about something doesn't make it come true. If you have a goal, you will strive toward achieving it. Goals provide results, whilst dreams do not.

Here are three suggestions for setting objectives.

Consider Your Passions

Choosing your values and your motivators should be a step in the process of creating life objectives. You should be passionate about your goals if you want to achieve them in the long run. Your objectives should have personal significance for you and make you feel proud after achieving them.

Set Manageable Objectives.

If your goal depends on something outside of you, you won't be able to control whether or not you achieve it.

Your personal goals shouldn't be dependent on other people. Additionally, they shouldn't rely on other factors that are out of their control.

Be truthful to yourself. Determine what you can control and what you cannot.

Write Them Down

Instead of just thinking about your objectives, put pen to paper and record them. Your objectives become more attainable and seem more realistic as a result.

Make a Plan

Now that you know what you're aiming for, it is time to decide how you're going to get there.

You should specify the precise actions you must take to achieve your goals. You can keep on track if you have a plan of action. As you complete each item on your list, cross it off to keep track of your progress and to see how far you still have to go.

4.2

How to Manage Time?

Each of us has 24 hours in a day. However, why is it that certain people seem to utilize every bit of their day? They don't have the ability to slow time down, despite popular belief. They are aware of how to effectively manage their time, though.

By practicing time management, you can succeed in your education, prosper at work, and experience less daily stress. Can you be sure that you are handling your routine well?

Audit Your Time

Finding out where you actually spend your time is the most crucial step you need to take when it comes to time management.

Downloading an application like Toggl, RescueTime, or your Calendar to log your week is the simplest method to keep track of your time.

Determine Your Peak Productivity Periods

Different people are productive at various times of the day. You can better plan your time by being aware of when you can work most productively. For instance, try to finish most of your work in the morning if you tend to be more productive then. At night, you can relax and indulge in your favorite peaceful activities.

Plan Your Day in the First 30 Minutes of the Day

Making a strategy for the day in the morning can be beneficial. As soon as you stand up, consider what has to be done and make a rough schedule for when to do it. Remember your errands, social commitments, and work duties.

Rank Your Tasks according to Significance

Before beginning your day's work, set priorities for your duties. To-do lists are a great tool, but instead of just listing everything that needs to be done, organize them a little.

4.3 How to Organize?

According to research, numerous areas of development can benefit from organization. We note increased rates of distraction and tension when things are disorganized. Teens that struggle with organization face more academic difficulties, get lower grades and communicate poorly with teachers.

Prioritize

You must multitask while working and studying. While multitasking, it's important to keep in mind the deadlines and significance of each task. A log must be kept, and one must act accordingly. When someone is aware of the deadlines and weight associated with a task they understand its due importance. Consequently, setting priorities is a crucial organizational ability that we all need to have.

Keep from Procrastinating

This could be considered a quiet killer. Never make the decision to wait until the very last minute. There are instances when one might succeed in doing so. But this is not a promise; if it becomes a habit, it might be harmful.

Establish and Follow Schedules

We can stay organized in the greatest way possible by making sure we follow a set schedule. However, avoiding overestimating the working capacity while creating a schedule is crucial. Working in a balanced way makes sure that you won't eventually burn out.

Be Self-Driven and Inventive

Being resourceful means having the capacity to overcome challenges or restrictions. This entails confronting challenges head-on and maximizing resources to address the issues. One needs to be sure to be resourceful if they are to keep these setbacks from disrupting the planned flow of work.

Keep Documents Up to Date

It is advisable to keep the completed work in an organized manner to prevent redoing work and make it simple to access previously completed work. When trying to get more organized, a smart place to start is by filing paperwork and backing up assignments. Organizing your work by dates and organizing your files by subjects are just a few simple strategies to ensure that your documents are stored effectively.

How to Improve Your Memory?

Our brains have an infinite amount of memory. The challenge is recalling or retrieving the information stored in our minds. Here are some tips for you:

Utilize Visual Association

This memory trick functions for two reasons. You will be more successful at retaining information if you engage more senses when learning or storing it. Visual cues are easier for us to remember than spoken cues.

Consider the scenario when you have a paper that needs to be turned in by 10 a.m. By picturing your suggestion placed on an alarm clock that reads "10 a.m.," you can memorize your assignment. In this case, it's important to paint an image that is as vivid as possible. Concentrate on an alarm clock that is flashing the time and beeping the alarm in your thoughts, making it seem extremely real.

Establish Routines

If you create a daily pattern for yourself in the areas where your memory recall is poor, you'll probably remember things better. If you have a bad habit of losing your keys, consider creating a system where you hang them on a hook by your front door as soon as you get inside your house.

Use the Chunking Approach

As a memory trick, our brains use chunking to divide up large amounts of information into smaller, easier-to-process chunks. The three main stages of chunking are grouping, seeing patterns, and organizing data by significance. For instance, it might be more useful to memorize a phone number in three separate chunks as opposed to one continuous string of numbers.

Speak to Yourself

It may seem strange to talk to yourself about the facts you are trying to learn, but it can be a helpful memory enhancer. Try expressing information rather than merely underlining or rereading it.

4.5
How to Multitask and be Good at It?

Does it seem that focusing on one item at a time is no longer sufficient? While multitasking can help you save time, it isn't always necessary. Multitasking needs to be done carefully and attentively to be effective. Remember, multitasking is not always bad. It is bad when you do it wrong or at the wrong time.

One must master the skill of multitasking in order to finish the required work in less time. Although multitasking may be challenging to master, it can increase productivity once mastered.

Let's see how you can excel at this skill.

Set Reasonable Objectives for Yourself

Overcommitting yourself might result in unneeded tension and worry. Make sure to give yourself attainable goals so that you won't feel defeated if you can't get everything crossed off your enormous to-do list.

Separate Important from Urgent Issues

One of the secrets to effective multitasking is to have a perfect to-do list. And the key to doing so is having a clear knowledge of the distinctions between significant (long-term sustainability) and urgent (tight deadlines) issues. Your to-do list's tone is determined by how important the task is, not by how urgent it is.

Do not Be Distracted

You should be aware that you are already multitasking, even if you believe you cannot. Check the setting where you work. There may be some noise, such as ringing phones or background music, or you might receive frequent app notifications.

Try a test to discover an efficient medium:

- Make a list of all external influences.
- Eliminate them one at a time, such as by switching your work location or disabling app notifications.
- Watch how their absence affects your work.

Set Aside Time to Focus Entirely on Challenging or Time-Consuming Tasks

Make it known that you would prefer to spend an hour or two alone each day, using that time to focus completely on challenging work.

Plan Ahead

Be ready early if you anticipate there will be significant pressure for work in the afternoon. Working ahead is demonstrated well if you've ever witnessed restaurant personnel wrapping flatware in napkins at 3 o'clock in the afternoon.

4.6 How to be Self-Resistant?

Self-control is the ability to restrain natural desires and prevent them from manifesting fully in behavior. There are instances when we must plan ahead and hold off on acting impulsively. We have the capacity to "shut down" our urges through self-control. But what good is a lock without the corresponding key? It's crucial to maintain our ability to speak or act boldly for the benefit of others or ourselves while exercising self-control.

Boosting self-restraint is similar to eating an elephant one mouthful at a time. The good news is that practicing restraint in one area can help you do it in others.

Be Self-Aware

Use your body to downshift when you notice a "rising" in the river of your emotions: Take three deep breaths. Put a hold on all snap decisions. Make time for clear thinking so that you can select positive words and deeds. Being aware of where you need to exercise greater restraint is the first step toward change. Don't "waste" your supply of restraint by making unnecessary demands of your daily routines at home and at work.

Assess the Scenario

Make a list of what "sets off" the issue or circumstance, listen to what is being said, and think. It can take a few seconds to several days to sort through your feelings in order to respond with confidence and objectivity, but practice makes one perfect! When it's possible, choose your response in preparation rather than reacting.

Align Your Behavior with Values

Look within to discover who you are and what you actually desire. What do you love? Is this the best? Which attitudes and behaviors will lead you there? What you're about to do or say does it represent who you are or who you want to be? How will these actions improve your relationships, productivity, and happiness? Are you going to choose to work on these? How? When?

Discipline Your Response

Choose which uplifting phrases or deeds you want to implement, enticed by the higher pleasure of your "desire" power. Even a coach can be hired to assist you in your training. You can develop a sense of control over your life via practice, giving you the ultimate freedom to regularly make decisions that result in positive consequences. You have the ability to follow your will.

4.7 How to Concentrate?

If you have ever struggled to finish a demanding assignment at work, study for a significant exam, or put in the necessary time on a complex project, you may have wished you had more focus.

The mental effort you put into whatever you're currently working on or learning is referred to as concentration. Attention span is occasionally mistaken with it. However, it refers to how long you can focus on one subject.

Connect with Nature

When it comes to honing your cognitive abilities, green space is essential. Among other advantages, spending time in nature may enhance your attention span and memory. For cognitive benefits, you can thank a range of outside stimuli, including the scent of flowers and the sight of lush green trees. So, wherever possible, try to take your breaks outside.

Decide to Concentrate on the Present

It could seem counterintuitive when you're having difficulties focusing, but remember that you get to choose where you focus your attention. It is challenging to focus when your mind is continually wandering to the past or the future. Make an effort to let go of the past, even if it's challenging. Allow it to go after acknowledging the impact, your feelings, and the lessons you've learned. Similar to this, decide to let go of your fears about the future after acknowledging them and seeing how they are manifesting in your body. We want to practice focusing on the details of what is crucial at this moment by employing our mental capabilities.

Practice being Mindful

To maintain present-moment focus, practice mindfulness. It entails impartially monitoring your thoughts, feelings, and surroundings. Additionally, it has been demonstrated to reduce stress, enhance working memory, and heighten alertness.

Train Your Brain

Evidence for the effectiveness of brain training exercises in improving adults' cognitive capacities, especially concentration, is beginning to accumulate in scientific studies. Playing these brain-training games may improve your skills of processing, problem-solving, working and short-term memory. Sudoku, Jigsaw puzzles, chess, and other brain-challenging video games are a few examples of these games.

How to Manage Stress?

Let's face it. Life can occasionally be tough. And stress doesn't always result from major events. Stress can also be brought on by the annoyances, demands, and pressures of daily life.

Maintain a Healthy Balance between Work and Play

Make time to complete your responsibilities and reach your goals (like schoolwork, chores, or practice). However, make time for the activities you enjoy as well (like working out, playing music, spending time with friends or playing with a pet.) The everyday practice of unwinding reduces stress.

Utilize the Positive Energy of Stress

Don't put off finishing work until the last minute. Furthermore, giving your best effort while rushing is challenging. Instead, utilize stress as motivation to complete a task. If you have a deadline, give yourself a strong mental push. Tell yourself, "OK, I've got this; I'm on it." Start immediately after that.

Eat Healthfully and Avoid Intoxicants and Stimulants

Nicotine, Caffeine, and alcohol all have negative health impacts and may even make stress worse over time, despite the fact that they may temporarily decrease it. The best place to start is with a healthy breakfast, then add more organic fruits and vegetables, less processed food, less sugar, and more water. Body performance is improved by proper nutrition.

Speak to Yourself about It

Sometimes it is not possible to phone a friend. If so, speaking gently to yourself might be a good alternative.

Just explain to yourself why you're anxious, what needs to be done to finish the task at hand, and most importantly, that everything will be fine. Don't worry about coming across as insane.

Play Music

Take a moment and listen to soothing music if a stressful scenario makes you feel overwhelmed. Playing soothing music helps lower blood pressure and reduces cortisol, a hormone associated with stress, and has favorable effects on the brain and body.

How to Cope with Failure?

It's only natural to feel hurt and unhappy after failing to accomplish a goal, small or big, but there's little use in dwelling on the past. These days, too many individuals try too hard to avoid failing, which only makes their lives more difficult.

Let's have a look at some efficient methods for overcoming the pain of failure so you can focus on moving forward with your life.

Be Nice to Yourself

When anything goes wrong, it's common to start criticizing oneself. You take your failure as proof that you are unintelligent, useless, or inadequate. This only makes you feel worse. Stop if this is you. Consider for a moment how you would help a friend through the setback you have encountered.

Keep in Mind that Everyone Fails

It can be all too tempting to fall into self-pity when things go wrong and ask, "Why does this always happen to me?" playing continuously in your head. Everyone makes blunders. Everybody experiences awful things once in a while.

Embrace Your Pain

It's critical to express your emotions. Allow yourself to experience anger, sadness, and disappointment when things go wrong. These emotions won't go away if you try to stifle them with phoney bravado; they'll just come back stronger and bigger the next day. Take them out immediately. Write about your emotions or confide in a close friend.

Take a Cue from Failures that Resulted in Success

History is replete with instances of both men and women who, after having failed once or twice, went on to excel in their chosen industries. They all had the characteristic of not letting setbacks stop them from experimenting and trying out new things.

How to Boost Cognitive Flexibility?

Cognitive flexibility is the ability to shift from one task to another or to consider numerous concepts at once. Cognitive flexibility is essential in both educational and professional settings because it promotes quicker learning, more inventive problem-solving, and better adaptation and response to novel situations.

Change Your Routine

If you're searching for a quick strategy to begin increasing your cognitive flexibility, try switching up your routine and approaching common tasks in a new way. You can create and strengthen new brain connections by even making the simplest adjustments, such as shifting your seat at the dinner table or brushing your teeth with your left hand rather than your right.

Think Creatively by Practicing

Making an attempt to think unconventionally and creatively or engaging in divergent thinking are other approaches to developing cognitive flexibility. Divergent thinking aims to produce a variety of thoughts on a subject in a short amount of time. It entails dissecting a subject into its component elements in order to obtain an understanding of the subject's different facets. Divergent thinking includes thinking in terms of limitless possibilities rather than finite options, and it typically happens spontaneously and freely.

Look for New Encounters

Every time you encounter an uncommon situation or learn something new, your brain creates new synaptic connections. Dopamine has been shown to be released in reaction to new and intriguing events, which enhances motivation, memory, and learning.

Make an Effort to Network with New People

You can become less dogmatic in your thinking and more open to the possibility that there may be more than one "correct" way of viewing things by getting to know people from various cultures and walks of life whose opinions and viewpoints are likely to differ from your own.

4.11 How to Visualize?

Develop your ability to see the future. Motivation and inspiration are driven by a strong imagination that allows you to see yourself clearly in your future success. Great goal-setters take the time to carefully picture themselves in the future after achieving this success.

Your mind experiences cognitive dissonance when you visualize future prosperity. Because the mind dislikes it when thinking and reality diverge, it starts to take action to alter reality, which encourages unconscious thought and helps you achieve your goals more quickly.

Clearly Describe What You Want Using All Five Senses

As you include more sensory images, your vision will become more tangible. And you'll be more motivated to take action to make the change.

Keep on Adding More Details

Think on the emotions connected to the result. If you can imagine how it will feel to reach the objective, you'll be more persuaded that it can be done. The more likely you are to act, the better.

Take Daily Action towards Your Goal

Recognize that challenges will come up. So that you may continue advancing toward your goal, close your eyes and make a plan for how you'll handle difficulties when they present themselves.

Become Knowledgeable

If you need more details, consult experts and do some study. Use this data to provide more detail on your vision statement and the steps required to realize it.

Think about Your Visualization for Some Time

Visualize for a total of 10 minutes twice daily. It functions most effectively just after you wake up and just before you go to sleep. This will motivate the unconscious to aid in your determined attempts to reach your goal.

Put your eyes closed and visualize the desired result with all associated senses and feelings.

On an index card, write your desired outcome as though it already happened. Read it both in the morning and at night.

Make a vision board and place it where you can see it every day. Study it before going to bed.

4.12 How to be Productive?

Being productive does not need slaving away at your computer for lengthy stretches of time each day or working long hours. To make the most use of your time, you must be wise about how you spend it.

Find out how to be more productive and how making the most of your time may improve your well-being.

Every Day, Wake Up at the Same Hour

One of the best strategies to continue being productive is to establish a routine. Maintaining a routine can help you remain disciplined and as alert as possible because it's less intimidating to start your day when you know what to expect, regardless of what you have on your plate.

Set the Tone by Treating Yourself Nicely

Your morning routine should consist of whatever makes you feel calm, motivated, and invigorated, whether that's a 30-minute yoga class, journaling, reading, or making a healthy meal.

Start Each Day with a Plan

Make a prioritized to-do list before you go to work in the morning. The difficult tasks are simple to put off and put off, but if you succeed, you'll have the confidence and drive to complete the remainder of your list.

The difficult tasks are simple to put off and put off, but if you succeed, you'll have the confidence and drive to complete the remainder of your list.

Be Mindful When Switching Tasks

Take a moment after completing your responsibilities, for instance, to consider how you would like to spend time with your loved ones—whether it be by sharing your day, watching a movie, or getting to know one other even better.

Make a List of Your Successes

Make a note of your day's accomplishments at the end of the day to be kind to yourself rather than dwelling on the work that still needs to be done.

How to Find Your Inner Zen?

Zen is merely another way of saying that you are "in joy, your sweet spot, or the moment." Many of us seek out life's high points in order to experience this emotion, which is frequently accompanied by an adrenaline rush and leaves us feeling serene on the outside. What if the situation was reversed, and you had easy access to this internal sweet spot? This way, it's more about what you're enhancing internally and less about what's going on outside you. This skill will help you keep your head clear while you turn your dreams into reality.

A straightforward daily practice of self-connection can help you achieve internal Zen.

Clean Up Your Life

Although removing clutter from our life may seem overwhelming, chaos only causes tension and may even cause resentment. Start small while decluttering your space, but don't overlook the significance of addressing your primary problems. Things will start to fall into place over time, and as you make progress, the process will seem less daunting.

Realize the Power of Yoga

Yoga not only replenishes your energy and fortifies your body, but it also aids in mind healing and promotes tranquility and peace. Yoga can help you get more in sync with your body, which will help you spot when stress is beginning to set in. Yoga is a terrific approach to reconnecting with your inner self.

Find a Happy Place

Your happy place may be cuddled up on the couch with a book in hand or on a strenuous climb through stunning scenery. Find what relaxes you, clears your mind, and makes you feel calm and at peace.

Shut Your Eyes

By closing your eyes, you temporarily block off the outside world and discover who you really are. Taking those moments to oneself is a lovely thing. You can help yourself by doing this and breathing deeply and slowly to help you regain your balance.
Good luck with your achieving your dreams!

Do You Remember?

- How can you use visual association to remember something?
- How can you be self-aware?
- How can you train your mind to concentrate better?
- How can you process the pain of a failure?
- What is divergent thinking?
- What happens inside your brain when you have new experiences?
- What is the first step in visualizing?
- What is your happy place?

CHAPTER 05

PACK YOUR BAG FOR A BETTER FUTURE

The first time leaving home is a significant milestone and should be exciting.

When someone first moves away from home, they may experience various emotions. It doesn't matter if you're leaving for school or work or just to escape your hovering parents—this is a major milestone that may be accompanied by excitement, anxiety, and some degree of confusion.

Nevertheless, before you make this significant choice, consider the following queries:

Are you able to manage the cost of paying your rent and other expenses?

Do you take on new challenges well?

Do you wish to explore relationships and activities that aren't possible for you where you now live?

But things aren't usually so straightforward. Consider delaying your decision if:

- Your desire to move out is motivated by peer pressure.
- You are absolutely unable to afford to move out.
- You are temporarily irritated with your family.

Let's include some skills to help you move out of your parent's home.

How to Find a College?

Best is code for toughest to get into when people refer to the "best" colleges. You may be sure that there are no top schools in the world. The ideal college for one person may not be ideal for another, and vice versa. There are some schools on any list—even among the most selective colleges and universities—that are a better fit for your academic interests, needs, and goals than others.

Make a List of Colleges

Create a list of institutions that interest you early on in the process by sitting down with your parents/guardians or a trusted adult, such as your school guidance counsellor. Both local and out-of-state public and private schools may be on this list.

Before choosing a choice, you should think about a range of experiences and results. This list should ideally contain 10 to 15 universities, all of which should have majors that fit your interests and career objectives.

Rank Your Needs and Wants

Your initial list of schools can be reduced by being aware of what you want and need from the college experience. For example, you could wish to experience the Big 10 with a sizable student body and lots of campus events. As an alternative, a smaller campus with a liberal arts foundation might be a better fit for your requirements.

Compare Offers of Financial Aid

You must hold off on applying until you get acceptance and financial aid award letters from the universities on your shortlist.

Consider the Benefits and Drawbacks of Each College

It's important to sit down with a trusted counsellor after completing the aforementioned stages to analyze the benefits and drawbacks of each college and determine which one best fits your requirements. For instance, the school with the highest financial aid package can have the lowest debt requirements, but what if the campus environment isn't right for you?

You can choose your college and locate the school that is the right fit for you by gathering enough information about your target institutions.

5.2

How to Know the Cost of Moving Out?

You need to take into account the expense of moving out too, which can quickly mount up. You could have to pay for kitchen supplies, furniture for your new home, and other costs. Save for the following things:

- Furniture, decor, and kitchenware ($1000–$3500): Purchase used items or search for affordable or occasionally free furniture in the local classifieds, on eBay, or on Craigslist.
- Costs of any setup ($500): For connection, some utility companies and internet service providers may demand a fee.
- Rental security deposit: This is often four weeks' worth of rent, and if you haven't damaged anything, you'll get it back when you leave.
- Rent for four weeks, once more: Plan for this as well since many landlords prefer to receive the first four weeks' rent in advance.
- Moving expenses: Will you need moving services, or can you enlist the aid of friends and family?
- You'll need an additional $500–$1000 to cover any unforeseen costs.

Depending on where you're renting and how much you're prepared to spend on furniture and furnishings, this might total up to $3000 or more.

Now that you know the amount, you can plan how you're going to save it:

- Consider how much you have already saved and deduct it from the amount you still need to. For instance, if you have $1,000 in savings and $4000 in moving expenses, you only need to save $3,000.
- Divide the remaining amount by the number of weeks or months until your move-in date. For example, if you want to relocate in six months, you'll need to save $3000 split by six, which works out to $500 per month or roughly $115 per week.
- By the end of six months, you'll be prepared to move into your own place if you start putting this much money each week into your savings account!

What You Need to Consider When Making a Budget?

By making and adhering to a monthly budget, you may prove to your parents that you know how to move out in a responsible manner. Here is a short list of things you should probably note:

Debt

Many individuals who are moving out on their own for the first time must pay off some form of debt. The majority of the time, it comes from student financial aid loans. Include these amounts in your budget without fail.

Rent

Your rent expense will likely be your biggest outlay of funds. To avoid rent hikes, try to sign a 1- or 2-year lease. Naturally, consider whether you'll need to leave before that. Try not to spend more than 30% of your salary on rent if you don't have to. This is another crucial maxim.

Meals

Most individuals overlook the cost of food. Although it might not be one of your bigger outlays, food is a vital expense. By preparing your own meals, you can reduce your food expenses.

Utilities

Electricity, water, gas, cable TV, the internet, and other comparable services will be billed separately. Internet and cable often have set prices, while gas, water, and electricity are metered services. Depending on the locality, most people pay between $50 and $100 per month for their utilities.

Transportation

Flights, auto insurance, cab rides, and vehicle registration are some examples of transportation expenses. The vehicle you'll use every day should be the first thing you budget for. Calculate your fuel and insurance expenditures if you plan to drive to work. Try to estimate the cost of daily transit if you plan to take public transportation. Last but not least, try to allow a little more money in your budget to cover travel and transportation expenses (just in case you want to fly home for the weekend.)

Entertainment

Some people spend so much money on living expenses that they become "home-poor," which means they don't have any extra money for enjoyable activities like vacations, dating evenings, or spontaneous excursions. Budget for fun activities as well, and keep in mind that having fun doesn't necessarily require spending a lot of money.

Medical

Make sure to account for your personal health care plan in your budget if you have one. Additionally, you should account for prescription medicine and visit copays in your budget.

Memberships and Subscriptions

Establish a budget for your streaming service, magazine, and gym memberships.

Toiletries and Clothing

Many first-time renters overlook setting aside money for clothing and hygiene. Make sure to factor in the cost of clothing as well as the price of soap, shampoo etc.

How to Make a Realistic Budget?

Although there are numerous websites that track your budget for you automatically, like Mint, I feel that using spreadsheet programs like Excel is the easiest method to lay out a budget.

Make a list of your important spending first, which should include things like rent, insurance, utilities, groceries, prepaid phone credit, internet, and transportation. Some of these expenses might not apply to you, but you can still add and remove them as necessary.

These categories are listed in their own row on the spreadsheet's left-hand side when I create a budget worksheet. If you live with roommates, divide your spending into two categories: shared expenses, like rent, and individual expenses, like transportation.

You should then include the weekly costs for each category in the column across from that.

- You should be aware of the costs like cell phone and transportation.
- You may find out how much the rent is by looking up the prices of homes and flats in the neighborhood you like.
- Plan to spend $200 each month on utilities.
- Find out the cost of renter's insurance (yes, you need it; it's worth spending $150 a year in case someone steals your belongings or the house) by researching insurance policies.
- Find the greatest price among internet service providers by researching them, then note their cost.
- Budget between $50 to $150 a week for groceries because prices vary depending on where you live and how much you consume.

You might need to change from one-time period to another (for instance, from weekly to monthly):

- Weekly to annual conversion: 52
- Weekly to monthly conversion: 4.33

Once you have entered all the numbers, add a row named total and sum them all up using the SUM function. Add up all of your personal expenses, divide any shared costs among the contributors, and there you have it. You must be earning this much each week.

What to Pack for Living in a Dorm or an Apartment?

When you pack for your new life in the dorm, there are some essentials you should remember to include. This list is not exhaustive since there will be items that are particular to you that you will vehemently refuse to part with. Likewise, you might not even need any of the things on this list. Start with the fundamentals, then make revisions as you go.

Large Items

To get a list of what is allowed and what is not, you must get in touch with the school. Depending on the available space, different colleges will have different policies regarding larger objects.

Desks, beds, chairs, and wardrobes are typically included with dorm furnishings. Here are some important factors to think about:

- Video game consoles and televisions
- A mini-fridge and microwave
- Additional sitting options like bean bag chairs and fold-out stools

Clothing

You should pack garments that can accommodate a range of temperatures and weather patterns depending on the climate.

You should pack pajamas, shorts, undergarments, long and short sleeve t-shirts, and jeans. Additionally, you might desire swimwear and at least one formal attire. Bring any necessary athletic clothing if you participate in sports.

Winter boots, a warm parka, gloves, and a cap are required for cold weather. An umbrella and a raincoat will be useful in damp areas.

Important Items

Several items are very necessary when settling into your new dorm room. The must-have items that you must either buy or bring from home are listed below:

It is essential to have bedding, including sheets, mattress covers, pillows, and a cozy comforter. You could need more blankets depending on the weather. Make your bed as comfy as you can because that is one thing you will desire when you are away from home. The digital necessities also include your laptops, smartphones, printers, and tablets.

If allowed, accessories like a small area rug, filing cabinet, wastebasket, and fan can help the room feel more comfortable.

Toiletries

Shampoos, conditioners, soaps, deodorants, toothbrushes, and toothpaste are among the essential toiletries. Some kids, especially girls, have extensive makeup collections that they don't want to part with. You could invest in a portable cosmetics caddy that you can take to and from the bathrooms in order to keep things tidy. It will be simple to get ready for class now.

You'll also need a robe for the shower, some flip-flops, and towels. You should also include any heat-styling appliances you use, such as hair dryers.

Random Things

Let's not overlook some basic necessities that we often take for granted. I can think of cleaning materials, laundry detergent, and change for the washing and dryer. Additionally, you should pack enough plastic cups, plates, and utensils for late-night munchies, as well as enough hangers for your closet.

Additionally, you might want some extra toilet paper in case the common restroom runs out. Also likely to be useful are trash bags, Kleenex, a first aid kit, necessary equipment, and a pair of scissors.

The same guide can be used for packing an apartment. Keep in mind you will have more flexibility to bring what you want but do not over pack.

How to Find an Apartment?

Although renting your first apartment can provide you with more freedom and flexibility, if you've never done it before, the procedure can seem difficult. It's not necessary to be. These recommendations can assist you in locating a location that satisfies both your needs and your apartment budget.

Choose a Price Range You Can Afford

Decide how much rent you can afford before you even start shopping for your first apartment.

Find the Neighborhood Where You Want to Live

The ideal location for you must be found. Finding an area, you like with activities and businesses you like should be included in this. Your school or place of employment should be close by when choosing the greatest area for you.

Determine If You Want a Roommate

Instead of renting a one-bedroom or studio apartment for yourself, you might discover that it is less expensive to split the rent for an apartment with numerous bedrooms. Calculate any potential savings and decide whether they are sufficient to offset the privacy loss.

Get Reliable References

When considering whether or not to rent an apartment to a potential tenant, many landlords place the greatest importance on the tenant's credit score. As a first-time renter, you might not have much credit history to rely on, which is why references are important.

Begin with 5 Properties

It's time to begin your search once you have chosen one or two regions where you want to live. Look online and in your neighborhood paper. You might want to take a trip around the neighborhood to search for any "for rent" signs because, in competitive housing markets, apartments may be rented before the listings are made public online. Make a few phone calls to different property management firms to learn what they have available.

Send the Application In

Once you have found an apartment you like, you'll need to submit an application, which very always entails a charge. Additionally, a lot of apps need consent to check your credit. The property manager can request a co-signer on your application if your credit isn't strong enough. As an alternative, you might need to put down a bigger security deposit.

Know What to Sign

When you sign a lease agreement, your living situation is official. You must sign up for any utilities like electricity, gas, water, and internet that are linked to the property.

Another renter may let you rent a portion of their home. If you haven't signed the lease, your living situation is unofficial.

Get a written agreement from the other tenants outlining your share of the costs of living and the amount of rent you'll be paying. If something goes wrong and you don't, you may not be able to get your money back.

Make sure you are aware of your obligations before signing anything. Learn more about leases and rental contracts.

5.7 What You Need to Know When Sharing with Flat mates?

Renting a home together can be less expensive than doing so alone. But make sure that you and your partner or roommates agree on duties right away.

Establish Ground Rules

Organize how you will each:

- Pay your bills, such as your rent and utility bills.
- Pay for the food.
- Leave the rental agreement (if one of you moves out)

Make sure to plan ahead and pay your electricity and rent bills on schedule. Your rental history and credit score may suffer if you don't make timely payments. You might even face eviction.

Finances Play a Role in Relationships

Discuss your finances with your partner if you plan to live together. Learn about one another's perspectives on money. Consider both your short-term and long-term financial objectives. You only need to start a conversation; you don't need to have everything worked out.

Knowing these things contributes to creating a solid basis for a positive relationship—both with each other and with money.

Get to Know Your Roommate's Schedule

After moving in with a new person, one of the things you should do is get acquainted with their schedule. This is crucial in relation to sleep schedules. If your roommate goes to bed at 9 p.m. and you remain up until 3 a.m. every night doing schoolwork with the light on, they won't be your biggest fans. Find a schedule that both of you can follow!

Be Considerate

Although this advice is a little generic, it's a sound guideline to follow when moving in with a new person. If you plan to have someone over, ask your roommate if it's okay. Don't take their meal without first getting their consent. In conclusion, be aware that you are sharing a space with someone else and consider their sentiments before making decisions!

What You Need to Know About Living in a Dorm?

The transition from your family home to the dorm can be challenging because it involves a complete change in your surroundings and social network. But if you know what to expect beforehand, you can make this experience simpler.

Continue reading to learn how to move to dorm life successfully.

Prepare for Random Roommates

Some people opt to share a room with a high school acquaintance or someone they met while visiting colleges. Take a chance and choose at random if it isn't in your plan. No need to worry; it's not entirely a gamble. Your school will email a link for roommate arrangements as soon as you opt to live on campus. You can enter your daily routines here, including when you wake up, go to bed, and whether you like a calm environment.

Try Out a Few Different Dorm Styles

You're sure to find a dorm style that matches your preferences among the many options available. There are single, double, triple, and quad rooms that can accommodate all of your housemates.

Put Social Media to Good Use

If you don't feel comfortable letting a machine choose your roommate, look for a potential roommate on social media and get in touch with them.

Leave the Door Open

You are essentially compelled to establish acquaintances in college. It's easy to make friends with your fellow apartment dwellers; you simply need to seize the chance.

Give Your Resident Assistant a Call

In college, you should get to know your resident advisor. Basically, your RA's role is to assist you in adjusting to college life. Your RA is the person you speak with if you're having problems with your roommates. Your RA will have helpful advice for you if you're experiencing problems adjusting to class.

How to Build Your Credit?

All of these items demand a solid credit score if you wish to buy a house, a new automobile, or a college loan. Therefore, obtaining these things will be a lot simpler if you establish credibility as a teenager.

Obtain a Secured Credit Card, Then Use It Sensibly.

Similar to a debit card, a secured credit card aids in credit building. Teens should consider it because they can open one without any credit history.

What you need to know about secured credit cards is as follows:

You must pay a deposit equal to your credit limit in order to open a secured card. (This often costs $200 to $500.)

Just like a conventional credit card, if you don't pay off your debt in full each month, interest will be applied.

You can switch to a typical unsecured credit card once your credit has grown.

In order to assist you in establishing credit, the bank reports each of your payments to the three credit bureaus. Therefore, in order to raise your credit score, you must make your payments on time and maintain a low balance.

Obtain Authorization to Use a Different Person's Credit Card

You can ask a parent or other relative if you can use their credit card as an authorized user if you aren't old enough to get your own.

Because you may benefit from their outstanding credit, this is an excellent approach to creating credit. Additionally, as they make timely payments and utilize the card, it will assist in establishing their credit history as well. Remember you will also be harmed if their financial situation is bad.

Get a Student Loan

Now, if you can avoid it, I advise against taking out a student loan. But there is good news if you must borrow one to pay for your college education: student loans really help you establish a credit history.

5.10
How to Deal with Homesickness?

Being homesick is a want for familiarity. College, moving into your first house or apartment, or any other form of shift, is frequent. It is pervasive and can be life-altering for some. Anxiety, grief, and dread are all typical reactions to leaving familiar surroundings for the unfamiliar and can all seem as symptoms of homesickness. Some people view it more broadly as a loss of the security and predictability of their chosen "home," wherever that may be.

Find Out How to Recognize Homesickness

Recurrent thoughts about home (such as the house, loved ones, motherland, food from home, or going home) are the hallmark of homesickness, and an impending or real separation from home is always the triggering stressor.

How can you tell whether you're depressed or anxious for a different reason rather than homesickness? Consider this: Am I dissatisfied because my circumstances are poor, or am I missing my former life?

Give It No Deadline

Before you even leave your old house and move into your new one, you might have homesickness. Sometimes you don't feel anything until you've been in your new home for a while and the novelty of your circumstance has started to wear off. However, regardless of when the sensations manifest, it's crucial to accept them for what they are.

Take Advantage of Nostalgia

In addition to the past, nostalgia also considers the future. Don't think that your present or future can't live up to what happened in the past. Instead, consider the best parts of what you've left behind and consider how you can duplicate them in your new environment.

5.11
How to Cope with Challenges in the Dorm?

Consider that your first semester of college is just two days away. Your parents deliver you to this odd, institutional-looking structure, assist you in bringing your stuff inside, and give you a big hug. Then they leave you behind and drive off. Welcome to dorm life. You are now on your own. Here are some recommendations to help you out:

Be Able to Tolerate Noise

Accept the fact that, in most cases, your neighbors won't be as quiet as you'd like them to be. Recognize that sometimes there isn't much you as an individual can do about that. Simply put, you'll have to learn how to deal with and ignore it. Try putting the music on a moderate volume and sitting as close to your speaker or phone as you can. You can tune out any loud noises coming from next door, thanks to this.

Go for a Privacy Signal

Together with your roommate, develop a "privacy signal." Sexual experimentation is common during the college years. In order to bring their lover there for a sexual encounter, you or your roommate may occasionally require some privacy in your room. Establishing a signal that the room is occupied and requires privacy is an excellent approach to ensure that neither of you interrupts the other in the middle of their exchange. You can hang a bandana, tie, or sock from the doorknob as a common fix.

Stay the Clean One

There is not a lot you can do to prevent the restrooms from being filthy because you are no longer living in the comfort of your home.

Buy a pair of shower shoes. Sandals or flip-flops also function. The bathrooms in dormitories aren't always the cleanest. Wearing shower shoes can help you avoid getting any of that shared scum on your feet.

5.12 How to Build Boundaries?

Whether you and your roommate are close friends or just roommates, dealing with roommate disputes may be extremely stressful and negatively impact your relationship, attitude, and capacity to unwind and relax.

That is why setting up clear limits is so crucial!

Know What You Need

The first step is to define the type of environment you wish to live in. You can ensure that you choose the correct roommate by taking the time to consider your needs in relation to the major issues that can lead to conflict (such as the division of duties or funds, cleanliness, noise levels, and guests).

Communicate

It should go without saying that communication is an essential component of this entire process. Early discussion of preferences, such as a need for privacy or financial planning, not only helps to avoid conflict but also makes it simpler to bring up a boundary when it is breached.

Work Together

Working together to find solutions and foresee future difficulties enhances the likelihood that both of you will respect limits and adhere to the plan, whether it be by coming up with a compromise that benefits both of you or by finding a solution that works equally well for both of you.

Be Respectful

Frustration might occasionally cause you to act in unexpected ways when you feel like you have no other choices. To make your point, you might speak louder or harsher, or you might withdraw because you decide it's not worth the effort. When living with a friend, how you handle the issue is even more crucial since you want to strike a balance between the friendship and your need for a comfortable space.

These skills will help you set on the path to independence!

Do You Remember?

- How can you calculate the cost of moving out?
- Name the things you need to consider when making a budget.
- How many dollars a month can you spend on utilities?
- Why do you need references when renting an apartment?
- What are two ways to build credit?
- What needs should you consider when building boundaries?

CHAPTER 06

HUNT FOR THE DOLLAR IN YOUR POCKET

It is better to begin planning for the future as soon as possible. This is a common experience for people entering adulthood when they have to make and process crucial financial decisions. But how can you select the best financial choices to make? Despite the fact that everyone's financial condition is different, the fundamental road to success is usually the same.

Gaining financial independence can give you more control over your money and, more significantly, over your life. Living within your means, exercising some thrift, and making sure that money is spent on essentials like food, shelter, and, yes, vacations are all crucial (relaxation is important, too, you know). You will be one step closer to being financially independent when you follow the steps below:

How to Create a CV?

You must highlight your abilities and academic accomplishments in a formal document, whether you're applying for summer employment, a part-time position, or even a work placement. When completing job applications, your resume is crucial, and writing one doesn't have to be tough.

Generally speaking, you should contain the following sections:

Header: This will start with your name and move on to contact information. Add your email address, phone number, and address. Your email-address should be business-like, contain both your name and last name, and be devoid of nicknames and slurs (for example, cutiepatootie41@email.com).

Summary: Because it serves as your sales presentation and is what potential employers will read first, the summary is very important. Here, you must briefly introduce yourself, your top skills and qualifications, and the position you're applying for.

Your educational background is listed here in reverse order. You should also include your educational grades are good, you may additionally add them.

Skills: Teenagers typically don't have a lot of professional experience, so you'll need to show off your skills in this section. Make sure your talents are appropriate for the position you're looking for.

Experience: When listing previous positions and pertinent experience in the field, be careful to include particular contributions you made, such as assisting a teammate or going above and beyond your duty call.

More sections: You are free to include any additional sections you deem necessary and appropriate. You might choose to add a part outlining your hobbies and interests, language abilities, or your business endeavors.

How to Find a Job?

Finding a job as a teenager might open up opportunities for you to gain experience, money, and references. The skills you gain in these settings will be useful while looking for a professional job following graduation. You can take the following actions, for example:

Explore Job Options

Teenagers are employed part-time by several organizations, corporations, and companies in various fields. Make a list of the topics and abilities that interest you, and then decide which positions are likely to be the best fit. Here are a few instances to think about:

If you enjoy cooking, you may search for positions in fast-food chains or hotels that might hire people without prior expertise.

You might look into local childcare programs or ask friends and family for babysitting jobs if you enjoy working with youngsters.

If you prefer being outside, consider applying for positions at construction firms, animal shelters, plant nurseries, and garden care businesses.

Consider looking for work at moving companies, vehicle washes, or commercial cleaning businesses if you want to stay active.

Obtain a Work Permit If Required

As long as you are over 13, you are eligible to work part-time, but if you are under 15, you may need a working permit. Teenagers must also have a Child Work Permit, which their employer must fill out and contain information about their responsibilities and working hours. Your school and your parent or guardian may also provide written permission for you to work.

Find Employment Opportunities Online

To find open employment in your neighborhood, search on internet job boards using your skills and interests. On some employment sites, you can also build a profile and upload your resume in order to be notified as soon as a position that matches your interests becomes available. It is also a good idea to frequently check the social media accounts of your favorite businesses, as some of them post job openings there.

Obtain References

References are a useful tool for demonstrating a strong work ethic. Consider requesting permission to use adults as references. You can speak with individuals who are familiar with you personally and your diligence. References from professors, coaches, and team captains are all highly recommended.

6.3
How to Fill Out a Job Application?

Send applications for the positions that interest you after completing your CV. Applying for several positions instead of just one and waiting for a response increases your chances of landing a job. You can even submit multiple applications to a company with many locations or job advertisements. Consider calling the recruiting manager after submitting your application online. During that conversation, you can also inquire about their review procedure.

Check up on your application. Follow up after five to seven days if you don't hear back from the company after sending your application. To find out your application's status and what to do next, you can phone the recruiting manager. Keep a spreadsheet up to date with the contacts for the locations you apply. In order to stay organized, you can also set reminders.

6.4

How to Develop Employability Skills?

Employers have recently expressed dissatisfaction with entry-level workers' lack of "soft" skills in a number of polls. Good listening, dependability, teamwork, conflict resolution, integrity and problem-solving are a few examples of soft talents. Since most teens do not have hard skills.

Employers look for the following categories of soft skills:

Communication

The term "communication" refers to a wide range of abilities, including public speaking, active listening, writing, and respectfully expressing opinions. You must be able to follow instructions correctly, read with comprehension, actively listen, talk and write in a way that other people can comprehend, and request clarification when necessary.

Teamwork

Businesses seek individuals who can develop relationships, work well in teams, contribute ideas and effort, and reach decisions together. Working well as a team includes having a cooperative attitude, a healthy regard for the perspectives of others, and an awareness that not every team member will be directly involved in leading the effort.

Positivity and Responsibility in the Workplace

Businesses respect employees that are driven to complete their work, complete projects on time, adhere to company rules, and exhibit honesty and dependability.

Professionalism

Professionalism is highly valued by businesses in their staff. Professional employees are punctual, considerate of others, present themselves neatly and impeccably, wear acceptable attire, and behave in a way that is appropriate for the job.

Employers expect young people to be able to solve problems on their own. When young persons are confident in their capacity to overcome problems, they won't pass up excellent possibilities out of fear. The best workers are capable of critical and creative thought, contribution, sharing of ideas and viewpoints, sound judgment, and decision-making.

Flexibility

Since no one is adept at foretelling the future, we really have no idea what the future holds for us. The workplace is no exception to the fact that the world is always changing. Even though layoffs, meeting new managers, or switching responsibilities can be daunting, workers who can roll with the punches typically succeed.

6.5 How to Prepare for a Job Interview?

Teens may find interview preparation to be somewhat frightening and tense, but it doesn't have to be that way. Employers who recruit teenagers don't anticipate you to have a large resume of skills, years of work experience, or a track record of success. Two words can encapsulate all they typically care about: a positive outlook.

They want you to be able to learn, to be dependable and on time, and to be willing to listen. You'll be an easy hire as long as you can convincingly demonstrate these skills in your interviews. Here's more insight for you:

Recognize Your Abilities

Think about your abilities and experience in relation to the requirements of the position before the interview. Make a list of your key accomplishments, talents, and strengths that you want to emphasize in the interview.

Establish Your Credentials

It's crucial to think about how your skills and experience complement the requirements listed in the job description before applying. This will enable you to more effectively and confidently articulate them during the interview.

Study the Company

By understanding the responsibilities and job description before the interview, you can anticipate the interviewer's queries. Furthermore, it could help you select the interviewer's own questions. Visit the company website to get conversation starters for your interview as well as more information about the company's history. The interviewer will see that you have taken the time to study about them and are interested in working for them if they hear you make references to your studies throughout the interview.

Memorize Your Resume

Knowing the specifics for each is crucial if you have prior work experience. As a result, you won't need to constantly refer to your printed resume when discussing each experience. Make a list of your job titles, the companies you've worked for, the dates you were there, and your duties.

Prepare Standard Interview Questions and Responses

The hiring manager will question you about broad and job-specific topics throughout the interview. To better understand their typical interview questions, do some online research or consult the Indeed Career Guide.

How to Manage Money?

If thinking about money fills your thoughts, you are not alone. 77% of respondents to a 2020 survey reported having financial worry.

Here are some immediate steps you may take to increase your self-assurance and enhance your financial management.

Make a List of Your Wants and Needs

Money can be spent readily. Making sensible financial decisions is not simple. Spending money largely on your needs rather than your wants is one strategy to help you manage your finances. Try to consider both your present demands and those you will have in the coming months. In one column, list the costs associated with what you need, and in another, list the prices associated with what you want. Consider the following questions: "Can I live without these wants? Are there any alternatives to my wants?"

Create a Saving Habit.

Young people can start a lifetime of healthy savings by starting to lay money aside for the future today. You don't even notice that you clean your teeth twice a day because it has become a good habit. Put some money away for the future now, when you have any income.

Learn about Investments and Savings

Few people ever become rich only because of their wages. Long-term prosperity is produced by savings and investments. Although the return on a savings account with a bank isn't very high, the money is liquid and secure, making it simple for you to use it to cover short-term expenses. Although the value of investments (bonds, stocks, and real estate) can vary substantially, they may eventually yield larger returns. In contrast to placing all of your funds in a savings account, which earns less than 1% interest, you can use investments such as stocks and bonds that could yield 4% to 6% annualized return if you have five to six years until college. Discuss how much a 4-year college education will cost with your parents if they haven't already created a 529 plan (college savings plan) for you. The money put into the plan can be invested, and withdrawals made later to meet approved expenses are tax-free.

Be a Savvy Consumer

Make a list of your weekly grocery needs and follow it to the letter. Use recipes that call for inexpensive, wholesome ingredients like tuna, eggs, beans, and lentils. To avoid making impulse purchases, eat first. Online pricing comparisons are especially useful for clothing and footwear. Enroll in college courses if they are free or inexpensive during high school. When the time comes for you to start looking for the right college, you will conduct more internet research, consult with counsellors, and tour a few institutions.

What is there to Learn about Personal Banking?

Learning to manage your own finances is a necessary component of being an independent teen, but it comes with a lot of responsibility. Having your own accounts can avoid check-cashing fees and other expensive financial services. Before registering an account, you must comprehend a few fundamental ideas.

- Create a savings account and let it alone. You would need to save less money per day to save the same amount of money the earlier you start saving.
- Some banks provide young customers with customized checking accounts that have lower fees and no minimum balance requirements.
- Checking your accounts' balances online on a regular basis will help you keep track of them.
- Never disclose your internet passwords or bank card PIN with anybody; memorize them.
- To prevent overspending, treat your debit card like cash whenever you make a purchase.

6.8 How to Find Side Gigs?

In the modern world, discovering some fantastic side hustles can help you earn some serious extra money or get a jump start on your life savings.

You can develop new talents, improve your financial literacy, and possibly even make a lot of money by side hustling. And if you do it correctly, it would not even get in the way of your participation in sports, school, or your social life.

Here are some tips for using side jobs to earn money as a teen.

Take Online Polls

You can earn quick money taking online surveys in your spare time or, at the very least, a few free gift cards! Several survey websites are available, and most of them let minors sign up. Swagbucks is open to anyone over the age of 13, while Branded Surveys and Survey Junkie are excellent choices for teens over the age of 16.

Find Odd Jobs Locally

Teenagers now have more access to odd jobs around town than ever. If you want to get serious about earning additional money this summer, download the Steady App and start looking for full-time, part-time, or gig work options.

Play Online Video Games

You can even get paid to play online games. That's correct!
Get rewarded for the time you waste by downloading an app like Rewarded Play!

Sell Your Unwanted or Outdated Items

There are many things in your closet that you seldom wear or that you outgrew last year. Perfect! Why not sell it to get some cash, either offline or online?
You can start selling the clothes you don't want by downloading the Poshmark or Depop apps to your phone.

6.9 How to Develop a Healthy Relationship with Money?

These actions will help you have a good relationship with money. Below are a few methods you can use.

Become More Transparent

Don't try to cover up any financial mistakes you may have made. Own up to it if you spent your entire allowance on something you didn't require. This makes it easier for you to hold yourself accountable and may allow others you share with to provide you with financial advice and helpful criticism.

Share Money Issues with Your Family

Feeling uneasy about the subject can result from treating money discussions as taboo or an issue that should only be discussed by grownups. Keeping your financial struggles to yourself might be counterproductive and lead to new financial problems.

Avoid Comparing Your Finances to those of Your Friends

Comparing your spending habits and purchases to those of others can provide erroneous results and an emotional reaction to financial issues. From their purchasing patterns to their entire financial condition, everyone is unique.

Do Not Feel Bad about Spending Money

You should not feel guilty about spending money on necessities even while you're focused on controlling your finances (or want). It's acceptable to treat yourself occasionally, and there are some purchases that must be made regardless of your budget.

6.10 What You Need to Know about Your Taxes?

It's critical to understand that you do not receive all of your money. You must pay taxes if you have a job and a source of income. Your take-home pay will be less than you might have expected because, in most cases, your employer will remove this immediately from your compensation.

At first, the idea of taxation may seem daunting. However, after you get the fundamentals, you'll know what to expect in terms of your compensation better.

Distinguish between Gross and Net Income.

Your gross income is your earnings before taxes. The amount remaining after taxes are taken out is your net income. It is the actual sum of money that you get to keep.

See if Your Income to See If It Is Tax-Exempt

Certain types of income exempt you from paying taxes. It typically takes the shape of gifts for teenagers.

Learn about the Income Tax Brackets

The tax rate you will pay on each component of your income is displayed in tax brackets. It's critical that you are aware of your tax obligations. Your income and method of earning it will affect this.

How to Invest Your Money?

Investing means putting money into something to make a larger profit down the road. A great way to manage your money is to use it to help you achieve bigger financial objectives like home ownership or retirement planning.

If you begin investing when you are still a teenager, time will be on your side and most likely result in a higher profit. According to Greenlight's survey on financial literacy, the majority of teenagers are interested in investing, but less than half don't pursue it because they don't know how. It is not as difficult as you might think to invest, but there are some important considerations.

Your success can be increased by being aware of the many sorts of advice and risks associated with investing. Start as soon as possible to maximize your earnings and expansion prospects.

Different Forms of Investments

By doing some research, you can learn about the various investments you can make, such as stocks, mutual funds, exchange-traded funds, or bonds. American Century Investments explain the contrasts between these classes.

Learn about Investing Apps.

Due to the risks involved with investing, people are reluctant. Trying out a micro-investing app is a good method to start slowly and understand how investments operate.

Find a Financial Advisor

Speaking with an expert is a smart choice if you're unsure about making investments on your own or want professional advice. A financial advisor can act as a sounding board for your financial decisions and help you manage your portfolio and make stock trades.

How to Avoid Debt?

Ideally, your spending should not exceed your income. Sometimes it cannot be avoided. The risk of starting to accrue debt increases. Two types of debt include mortgages and student loans that may really enhance your quality of life. Your mental health could eventually suffer if you are unable to regulate them. A low credit score from poorly handled debt can also lead to a poor credit history. Even while you might not be able to avoid falling into some debt, there are steps you can take to keep it from becoming out of control.

Instead of Using a Credit Card, Use a Debit Card

32% of teenagers are unable to distinguish between a debit card and a credit card. The latter is a loan because it enables you to loan money against a line of credit. You will be charged interest and late fees if you don't make your payment on time. With a debit card, you can make an immediate withdrawal from your bank account to complete the transaction.

Recognize Good Debt from Bad Debt

When you have good debt, the interest you pay is worth the loan's principal. For instance, a student loan enables you to pursue a degree that may result in a better career and increased earning potential. In contrast, using credit at your preferred apparel retailer and making long-term purchases can result in a drop in credit scores, and more.

Maintain a Good Credit Rating.

How you handle your money is reflected in your credit score. Your personal characteristics are scored, such as how frequently you make on-time payments, if you've missed any, and the total amount of your outstanding debt. Future decisions may be impacted by your credit history, such as whether you are approved for homeowner's or auto insurance.

Make Cautious Use of Your Credit Card

Possessing a credit card has benefits, including the ability to build good credit and eligibility for prizes or incentives. Using the card to make purchases that you can pay off in full within 30 days is a clever move. Never ever max out your card, and always pay your bills on time.

How to Get Your Bills in Order?

You can better budget your spending if you know that most of your money will go toward items like your internet, smartphone, power, water, car insurance, and other living expenses.

Many of these have inexpensive solutions, but you'll need to shop around to get the lowest prices (assuming you have a reliable income). Even if you already have a provider, you might want to switch because new clients frequently receive discounts.

A security deposit (rental bond), which often equals a few weeks' worth of rent, is typically required when you move into your first apartment or unit. Ask your parents for guidance about this.

How to Get Free Stuff?

When moving on a tight budget, furniture is one of the most expensive expenses. Thus many individuals decide to sell or even donate goods they don't want to move.

Joining local Facebook groups will show you how easy it is to find free items to decorate your home. For finding free items, other websites like Gumtree are also helpful.

Do not forget to enjoy your money!

Do You Remember?

- What should you include in the header portion of the CV?
- When do you need a work permit?
- What are soft skills?
- What have you learnt about investments in this chapter?
- Which websites can you use to find odd jobs?
- How can you differentiate between net and gross income?
- Why should you use a debit card instead of a credit card?

CHAPTER 07

YOUR FOUR WHEELS ON THE BLACK CARPET

The first car is something you never forget. The independence it affords is a thrilling rite of passage, whether you acquire the keys to a family hand-me-down on your 18th birthday or indulge yourself much later in life. However, picking and purchasing an automobile for the first time can be confusing. Which one is better, gasoline or diesel? Whether a manual or automatic? Here are our suggestions to help you get started on your motoring trip, whether you're ready to leave right away or are still debating your options. I know that the choice can be overwhelming.

How to Set Your Car Buying Budget?

Owning a car is now feasible, thanks to modern financing options, and the availability of quality used cars. You might be able to purchase an automobile that fulfils your needs if you have an extra $150 to $200 each month.

Determine a pricing range that you can afford to start with. Think about how much money you have in savings, how much money you make or can afford to pay each month and any ways you may reduce spending to put money toward a car.

The following considerations should be made when getting ready to buy a car:

- You'll save a lot of money on interest if you can afford to pay the entire amount upfront. You might even be able to get a deal.
- You can have problems getting financing because the majority of teenagers don't have credit records. You can get a loan through your bank, credit union, or even insurance, but you'll probably need a cosigner—perhaps a parent—who has a history of employment and good credit.
- Even with financing, upfront costs will still be the highest. When you buy a vehicle, you must pay fees for registration and titling. Additionally, your monthly payments will be reduced, the more money you can put down.
- Even though financing options differ, you can use this straightforward rule of thumb to calculate your monthly payment: for a 48-month loan, you'll need to pay around $25 per month for every $1,000 you borrow. Aim to keep payment schedules under 60 months. This calculator might be useful to you as well.
- Added costs associated with having a car, such as maintenance, gas, and insurance, should not be overlooked.

To find the most affordable choice for you, think about stopping by different financial institutions and car dealerships.

7.2 How to Find the Right Car?

Start your online search to find out what kind of car you can afford.

You must think about vehicle dependability and safety as a novice driver. Larger cars seem to be safer than smaller ones in general. A midsize sedan might be more crash-resistant than a compact car, and because of its low center of gravity, it is typically less prone to roll over. Additionally, seek vehicles that don't emphasize horsepower. Smaller, more efficient engines and drivetrains, as well as hybrid or electric vehicles, can promote safer driving while also lowering your insurance and fuel costs.

You'll also need to make certain trade-offs to find the perfect feature mix at the right price. A simple decision to make is whether to purchase anything new or used. Even while new cars are more expensive, they may come with safety features that aren't included in earlier models but are particularly useful for novice drivers, such as backup cameras and driver-assist systems like automated braking. A pre-owned automobile that has been certified is another option. It may cost more than other used cars, but it might have a limited warranty and cost less to insure.

Should You Get a Used or New Car?

The best safety features are undoubtedly found in the most recent vehicles. Many even start braking on their own if they sense an impending collision. Your lane drift will be monitored, and some of them may even gently nudge the vehicle back into position. Blind-spot monitoring, which frequently includes alarms if the driver tries to merge into another vehicle, can help drivers avoid issues in the event of brief attention lapses.

So, should you purchase a new vehicle? Really, it depends. Can you simply afford it, even paying for teen driver's insurance? Are you prepared to spend five figures on a vehicle that has a decent possibility of being totaled? A new car might be a good alternative if the answer to all the questions is yes.

But for many others, purchasing a used car is preferable. The cost will be reduced. Insurance will cost less. Registering could possibly be less expensive. Additionally, you might be able to obtain used components to replace the damaged ones if you do get into a collision, saving you even more money.

How to Pay for Your Car?

You'll need a parent or other responsible adult to own the automobile if you're under the legal age to do so in most nations. They can transfer the title to you whenever you achieve the required age. Take into account these popular payment methods to put yourself in control:

Get a Loan

You can obtain a loan if you are unable to pay the whole price of the vehicle. Only those at least 18 years old are legally permitted to obtain loans; even if you are, the lender will likely require a parent or other responsible adult to co-sign. However, you must make the payments on time each month to avoid damaging your credit or your cosigner's credit.

Buy It Right Now

With the money you've saved or assistance from a family member, you can cover the total cost of the vehicle.

Lease it Out

When you lease an automobile, you merely pay for the privilege of driving it; you don't actually own it. This may be a cost-effective approach to purchasing a modern vehicle. The number of kilometers you can drive is nevertheless restricted by the lease. (If you exceed, you'll be charged more.) And when the lease expires, you have to return the vehicle (or you can buy it then). Additionally, the dealer will bill you for any damage.

7.5 How to Negotiate at the Dealership?

The best way to find out what vehicles are offered in your area is to browse online. Most dealers allow you to schedule appointments and advertise their inventory on their websites.

The best way to find out what vehicles are offered in your area is to browse online. Most dealers allow you to schedule appointments and advertise their inventory on their websites.

Before making a purchase, it's crucial to get in the driver's seat of a potential car and test-drive it. Make sure the seat is adjustable, will fit in your garage, and can manage your daily activities.

However, you are not restricted to the nearby dealers. You can browse a nationwide inventory of used automobiles, thanks to online retailers like TrueCar, Carvana and Vroom. Without leaving your home, you may browse and apply for financing. After choosing a car, you have up to a week to test drive it and have a mechanic look it over.

Although negotiating can be scary, the key to getting the best bargain is speaking up for yourself. Bring any necessary papers, a solid grasp of your credit history, and the correct questions to ask. But the ultimate truth is that if you can't get the bargain you deserve, be ready to walk away.

When it's time to seal the sale, stick to your agreed-upon figure. The dealer will likely push for extra charges and add-ons.

How to Practice Basic Car Maintenance?

It's wonderful to finally have the independence and flexibility to operate your own automobile. But what about a breakdown on the side of the road and probable costly auto repairs? Not very good. Concentrating on good vehicle maintenance is one method to minimize expensive repairs. Here are a few fundamental actions to take that will simplify your life as a car owner.

Tire Pressure, Rotation and Tread

Tires are crucial for a car to operate safely. Tires that are under-inflated by more than 25% are three times more likely to cause an accident. Tire pressure may be easily checked with electronic tire gauges. Be sure you use it frequently and that you have one. Insert a dime to determine the tread depth on your tires. It's time to purchase new tires if you can see Abraham Lincoln's entire head. Spend some time to learn how to check the tread and tire pressure. Additionally, learn how to change a flat tire in practice. Rotating tires on a regular basis increases performance and extend tire life. According to Michelin, tires should be turned every six months or 6,000–8,000 miles.

Change the Oil

Modern engine oil additives that lessen wear-and-tear on the engine degrade after 3,000 miles and impair engine performance. You need to locate the dipstick in your bonnet. It is a small colored handle. Pull the dipstick out of its tube and see if the oil is below the low marked line.

Keep in Mind to Use the Lights

Vehicle lights are the only means of communicating with other motorists on the road, except for the horn. At least once a week, ideally at night, check the backup, brake, back and rear signal lights, and low and high beams.

Battery and Brakes

Make careful to check your brakes and battery every time you get your oil changed. The majority of roadside emergency services receive the most calls regarding no-starts. Ensure that there is no corrosion and that the connection is obvious. Given the significance of brakes, it is recommended to leave this crucial inspection to the experts. Brakes should be inspected every five months or 5,000 miles.

How to Practice Road Safety?

First-time driving lessons are both exciting and intimidating. I am aware of the frustrations connected to this significant life decision. Let's look at how we can make the transfer as painless and secure as we can.

Accelerate Slowly

Although it can be hard to resist the urge to slam on the gas as soon as the light turns green, self-control is crucial. When you gradually increase your speed, your engine operates more effectively. From a full stop, slowly begin to roll while applying more pressure to the gas pedal.

Brake Gently

The accelerator shouldn't be slammed all the way to the floor, just like when you're accelerating. One of the most crucial fundamentals a new driver can learn is how to know when to stop. As soon as you can, start lightly pressing the brakes if you notice a stop sign or the light in front of you turns yellow.

Until your car stops completely, apply the brake pedal gently and steadily.

Steadily Hold the Wheel

You maintain control of the vehicle with smooth steering. Maintaining a firm grip on the wheel when making curves or driving straight ahead is crucial.

Maintain a Safe Speed

It can be tempting to exceed the posted speed limits as you get more accustomed to driving. However, obeying the speed limit is important for your own safety as well as for others.

Engineers conduct comprehensive research to establish the speed limit. These engineers consider the type of route, the history of accidents, the volume of traffic, and visual distance. It is not worth risking your life or the lives of others to shorten your commute time.

Be Alert to Traffic Signs

Gain a thorough understanding of all pavement markings, safety signals, and traffic signs. Never disregard a traffic sign or a safety signal just because you feel comfortable with your driving skills. There is a reason why the signs are up.

Maintain a Safe Distance

Maintaining a sufficient "cushion" between yourself and the vehicle in front of you is crucial regardless of driving expertise. But because you're a new driver, your reaction time is naturally slower than other people's.

The "two-second rule" in which you leave a two second space between your car and the car in front of you will prevent you from hitting the automobile in front of you from behind, costing you more in insurance and repairs.

7.8

What to Do If Your Car Breaks Down?

It might be dangerous and inconvenient if your automobile breaks down while you're driving. The situation can get dangerous depending on where you are stuck on the road (after a turn, on the motorway, or on a route with little to no shoulder).

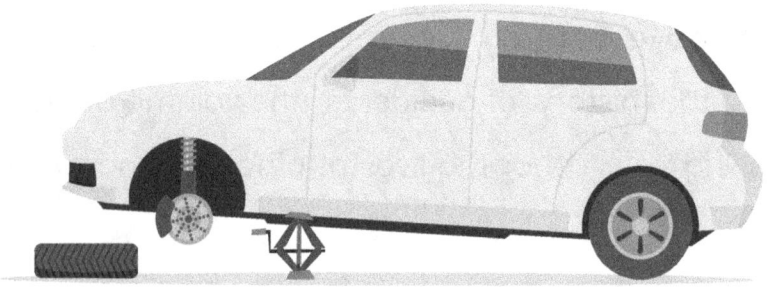

Get Ready to Stop

It's not always the simplest option to stop. You can be driving on a mountain road with little room for shoulders and lots of blind curves, or you might be on a busy interstate in a congested area.

However, try to evaluate your particular circumstance and choose a path of action. You must be careful as you try to get yourself safely out of traffic because until you move your car safely to the side of the road, your breakdown will disrupt other cars.

Turn on the Hazard Lights

Utilize your hazard lights to alert other drivers that you are in trouble, and use hand signals to move to the side of the road.

If you can, use the momentum of the car to drift to a safe area.

Pull Over to a Safe Spot

Once you've located a secure location, park the car normally while keeping the hazard lights on.

Lock the doors, turn off the ignition, and remain inside the car.

Make the police call yourself if you can. Roll down your window and ask anyone attempting to assist you to dial 911 if they want the police.

If your insurance policy includes roadside assistance, contact your insurance provider. If not, request a tow truck be sent.

Drive Your Vehicle to a Secure Area

Analyze the circumstances. Before making any judgments, you should always make the best assessment of your surroundings.

Identify the Issue

Make only the most fundamental evaluations of the car's condition. It can be quite helpful in this circumstance if you are familiar with the engine, but it's usually not the best moment to attack the issue head-on.

You can check for a loose power cable or blow a fuse under the hood, but anything more involved will likely be ineffective because you might not have access to the equipment and tools you typically need.

How to Navigate Your Ways?

It's always helpful to have a backup plan for emergencies or awkward circumstances. You'll have a little more peace of mind if you know how to navigate with a paper map. Additionally, paper maps are simple to use and beautiful to look at.

The essential components of a paper map

So, how exactly does one read a paper road map? The secret lies in comprehending the various components of a map and learning how they interact.

Index: Most maps provide an index, which is an alphabetical list of places. A city map, for instance, might include a street index and a list of significant landmarks. An index of notable towns and cities is likely to be present on a state map. In an atlas, the index is located at the rear. Each index entry has a number-letter combination (such as F6 or M14) next to it that stands in for a location on the map.

Compass Rose: A compass rose may be found on almost all paper maps, which serves as a visual cue to steer you in the right direction. On a map, the north is normally at the top. If you have a standard compass, align it with the compass rose on your map to better understand the direction to head.

Grid: Most maps are organized using a grid. A grid has rows of numbers across the bottom and columns of letters down one side of the page. This can help you locate any cities or streets mentioned in the index. To locate each location, you're looking for, trace right or left or from the letter and down or up from the number.

Scale: A scale is useful for route planning and determining how far you need to travel. A scale, or line marked in inches and labelled with distances, can be found on all decent maps. This displays the proportion of real distance to map distance. For instance, a distance of 1 inch on a map can correspond to 20 miles of actual distance. You have 120 miles to drive if you use a ruler and your map to measure 6 inches from your current location to your destination.

Topographic Features: Lines and shading are used on some maps, referred to as topographic maps, to show you the type of terrain you'll be driving over. A topographic map can help you locate mountains, valleys, hills, and other terrain features along your journey. Your map may utilize textures and colors to depict an area's elevation changes and significant geographic features, even if it isn't a topographic map.

Legend: All maps feature what is referred to as a legend. This function explains the meaning of each map sign, line, and color. You can distinguish between interstate highways and side routes, recognize rest areas and mountain peaks, find spots of interest, and much more with a map legend.

How to Keep Your Car Clean?

Even though you spend a lot of time in your car, you don't want to constantly thoroughly clean it. These seven suggestions can help you maintain your automobile clean every day.

Air Freshener

One underrated way to keep your car smelling clean and new is to use an air freshener. You don't need to dangle an air freshener from your rearview mirror because there are several companies that make air fresheners that attach to your vents so the air flowing out smells good!

Check Your Shoes for Dirt

The mess can stay outdoors, saving you the trouble of cleaning your car. Make an effort to remove any grime, mud, or snow from your shoes before entering.

Use Wet Wipes

To clean up a spill, you might need something more durable than restaurant napkins. By having a box of wet wipes in your car, you may easily clean while you're on the go.

Use a Garbage Can

Carry a dustbin with you at all times to avoid having to pick up trash afterwards. Whether it is a plastic bag or a portable trash container, there will be a designated location for it to go so that it is not scattered throughout the car. Just keep in mind to empty it once it's full!

Use Organizers

There are organizers designed to fit the backs of the front seats that may be used to keep games and other travel-related items organized while also preventing children from kicking the back of the seat. Purchase a shoe organizer or you can also buy your own. You can find center console compartments for the front seat's dividers.

Happy driving!

Do You Remember?

- What do you need to keep in mind while deciding on car buying budget?
- How to decide to get a used or new car?
- What are three ways to pay for your car?
- What are some ways you can do to drive safely?
- What are some ways to keep your car maintained in check?
- How can you handle a car emergency?

CHAPTER 08

WHEN SURFING THE WEB WATERS

One approach to make your residence secure is to lock the door. You can prevent theft of your bike by using a bike lock. Your treasured possessions are kept in a safe for protection. But how can you safeguard your online safety? I've put together a comprehensive internet safety guide with cybersecurity best practices and suggestions to keep you secure online.

How to Make Sure Your Internet Connection is Secure?

When you use a public Wi-Fi connection to browse the internet, you have no direct control over the security of the connection. Even if it's not always safe to use public Wi-Fi, you can avoid it when you're out and about. When using a public Wi-Fi network, refrain from performing private activities such as online banking or shopping. If you must do this, use a VPN, or virtual private network. A VPN will safeguard any data you send across an unreliable network. If you don't use a VPN, wait to conduct any private transactions until you have access to a dependable internet connection.

How to Use the Internet Mindfully?

The internet is the most fantastical, make-believe realm on earth, second only to Narnia. And because it's so magical, getting lost in it is quite simple. Distractions include food photos, kitten videos, pretty girls on Facebook, insightful articles about Barack Obama, and checking to see if anyone has liked your most recent tweet.

Here is a collection of techniques for using mindfulness when web browsing.

Set Boundaries: By letting the websites you visit fulfil the function you hired them for (informing you, entertaining you, connecting you with other people) instead of just something to stay on top of, you allow them to do what you pay them to do (entertain you, inform you, connect you with other people).

Slow Down: Moving more slowly gives your brain a better opportunity of comprehending what you are doing. Slowing down when you're online can seem like an odd strategy to increase productivity, but you'll probably end up spending less time on useless websites, which will save your valuable time.

Install an App to Assist You: Numerous Mac and PC apps are available that will play sounds or display messages to prompt you to pay attention, be aware of your actions, or take a break. For the Mac, I use BreakTime, while for the PC, the Insight Meditation Society suggests Mindful Clock. This website is compatible with any computer, and Break Reminder works well on PCs as well.

Think about It: Should I tell someone about this? Like the majority of individuals, there are a ton of silly photos of me online. And for every inane photo or video of mine that is circulating, there was the moment of stupidity that caused it to be posted in the first place. Although it may sound like cliché advice, it is important to consider whether what you spread or post will be shared publicly.

At the end of the day, using the internet to practice mindfulness requires setting an aim. It will be much simpler to practice mindfulness online if you set out to be aware of your activities as you perform them rather than automatically surfing.

On your journey to enlightenment, you're inevitably going to lose consciousness and fall into a black hole or two. But along the road, you'll save a ton of time and effort.

How to Check if a Link is Safe?

Before clicking on any links while browsing social media or reading your email, make sure you know and trust them.

Moving the mouse over a link might help determine whether it is secure. This will display a preview of the complete URL in the status bar of your web browser. Make sure the preview link points to the correct website by double-checking it on Google by typing the business name.

For instance, the link preview in an email from Wells Fargo bank that reads "www.wells-fargo-bank.com" does not correspond to the correct site URL that appears in Google, "www.wellsfargo.com."

You can view a preview of a link in your browser's status bar by moving your mouse over it in an email or on a website. Before you click, be sure it corresponds to the official firm site. Additionally, it's safer to go to the brand's official website to log in if you receive an email asking you to log in rather than clicking the login link in the email. You can access the official website by searching for the company name on Google or, if you know the URL off-by-heart, by entering the address directly into the browser's URL bar.

You can always call to confirm a request to log into your bank or other accounts in an email or on a website.

8.4 How to Choose Strong Passwords?

Passwords are one of the biggest cybersecurity weak areas. Passwords that are easy to remember are routinely chosen, which leaves people open to hackers. Additionally, if a hacker is able to obtain your login credentials from one website, they may be able to access other websites that utilize the same login, putting users at risk. Choose secure passwords that are challenging for attackers to crack. An effective password is:

- Long — at least 12 characters long, preferably more.
- A combination of characters, including capital and lowercase letters, symbols, and numerals.
- Avoid using obvious things, such as consecutive numerals ("1234"), or private information that might be assumed by someone who knows you, like your date of birth or the name of a pet.
- The use of distinctive keyboard shortcuts.

How to Recognize an Online Predator?

When they hide behind a computer screen, online predators can be difficult to spot at first since you don't know their motivations. It's quite challenging to tell whether you're genuinely speaking to someone of your age because they utilize false accounts, phoney profile images, and fake information. This guide can help you:

Online Predators Are Nice

Contrary to popular belief, cyber predators can present themselves as friendly people. The most dangerous ones, whether on social media or in an online chat room, don't seem false at all and genuinely engage in real talks with youngsters in a relaxed setting.

Online Predators Request Personal Data

They want information about you that they can use in future talks, such as your full name, birthday, residence, and the school you attend.

They might not always ask you direct questions like "Where do you go to school?" "I used to live in City X," they might casually bring up in conversation, "Many wonderful memories there."

Online Predators Want Private Conversations

Online bullies are constantly looking for one-on-one interactions where no one can hear or see what they are saying. Any platform might be used for this, including Skype, Google Hangouts, WhatsApp, and inbox messaging. It is important that the communication should be confidential.

Online Predators May Already have Information about You

They can know things about you that you did not tell them yourself. You could do this, for instance, by posting items on social media.

Online predators ALWAYS concur with your position. No matter what you say, they hold the same opinion. They take this action in an effort to win your full faith.

Online Predators Keep an Eye on Your Online Activity

Numerous cyber thieves will monitor your behavior for their own gain. They'll investigate you and find out more about your online habits. This involves determining your online availability and how frequently you post on particular websites.

Online Predators Make You Feel Special

They keep emphasizing how valuable you are to them. They'll compliment you on how attractive, funny, and/or intelligent you are. They will also express their delight at meeting you.

Online Predators Attempt to Turn You against Others

They will discount your relationships with other people in an effort to value your relationship with them. They'll tell you that your loved ones don't value or comprehend you in the same way they do.

Online Predators Desire to Catch You in a Vulnerable Situation.

Whenever they utter a phrase like "What's wrong?" Consider your words before you say anything to them, such as, "Tell me what's upsetting you."

These abusers enjoy hearing from you when anything makes you furious or depressed. By doing this, you create a sense of trust in their eyes.

Online Predators Will Make You Believe What They Are Doing is Normal

Do not allow them to persuade you that their actions are OK. If they are acting in a way that makes you uncomfortable, you are not at fault.

Stop talking to them right away and block them if you ever suspect you're conversing with an online predator. Do not be reluctant to seek assistance by informing a responsible adult if you believe a stranger is trying to stalk you online.

What to Do If You Get Hacked?

We're all vulnerable to hacking in a world that is becoming more and more computerized. Everyone shares personal information online, from passwords and identities to locations and bank card numbers, every day.

Often, it happens in unexpected ways. Personal social media sites, laptop or computer, and even linked devices like Alexa and Google Home can all be used to access your information.

Really, you run the danger of a hack if it's internet-based. The good news is that you can actually better defend yourself in this way.

Change Your Passwords

This is significant as hackers looking for any way in to a larger network may exploit weak passwords as a point of access. Make sure the passwords you use on accounts and devices that save sensitive data are strong, one-of-a-kind, and difficult to guess. It won't do to add your birthday to your mother's maiden name. You can rapidly create secure passwords for yourself with the help of a reliable password manager like LastPass.

Secure the Way You Log In.

Ensure your logins are just as safe after securing your passwords.

Two-factor authentication, available on most accounts, maybe something you've heard of. This additional safeguard makes sure you are the legitimate user of the account you're attempting to access.

Two-factor authentication functions as follows:

- Requesting your login information
- Sending a special, time-limited code to your mobile device through text or email that you must enter in order to complete the sign-in procedure

You might wish to prevent some third parties from accessing your information while you're at it on websites like Facebook, Twitter, and Google. To protect the information, you share, follow the instructions in the settings section of each website to turn off these authorizations.

Make Contact with those who can Provide Assistance

There are crucial actions to take immediately if you feel your bank information has been unlawfully accessed.

- Among them is contacting your bank. They will assist in processing claims and keep an eye out for questionable spending patterns.
- Let your trusted family and friends know of your suspicions so they can look out for phishing emails or other strange communications. Phishing, sometimes known as "fishing," is an attack that tries to steal your money or your identity by tricking you into disclosing personal information on websites that look official but are actually fraudulent.
- The Federal Trade Commission can assist with a recovery plan and crucial documents if you can demonstrate that you are a victim of identity theft.

Managing a potential hack is a serious matter. You can avoid the worst of it if you are informed, listen to your intuition, and take the required precautions.

How to Identify When You Are Being Catfished?

There is always a chance that you could be scammed, whether you're seeking love on an online dating site, making purchases on Facebook Marketplace, or searching for work on LinkedIn.

But how horrible is it really?

In 2021, imposter scams, in which fraudsters pose as someone they are not, were the second most prevalent kind of fraud. The Federal Trade Commission reports that this year, imposters stole more than $2.2 million (FTC.)

Let's discuss how to spot a fake dating account on the internet.

- They have a "perfect match" account — People with images fit for a magazine or who appear to be supermodels should be avoided. Catfishers will attempt to con you by using alluring images.
- Their social media profiles appear dubious – Sometimes, a romance scammer can build phoney social media profiles to make you think their dating profile is legitimate. No recent posts, a low friend count, or simply using the same photographs as on the dating site are all red flags to look out for. On Facebook, the typical user has 338 friends.
- They don't have a strong web presence – If you Google their name and discover little, you might be dealing with a fraudster.
- They make a powerful first impression and declare their love for you – Dating con artists will attempt to swiftly arouse your emotions. It can be fraud if they declare their love for you within a week or two and try to contact you outside of the platform.
- Scammers will frequently claim that their victims are in the military or employed by an international organization because they live far away and cannot visit. However, the inability to meet in person is a major red flag. This is particularly true if you are unable to see them during a video call.
- A fraudulent online dating account will simply message you; they won't engage in a video chat with you. They'll always have an excuse to cancel if you schedule a video chat, such as that they can't make it or that their webcam is malfunctioning.
- They make requests for money or assistance with family issues; catfishing frequently turns into financial fraud. Someone is certainly trying to convince you if they start requesting pricey gifts or money to cover unforeseen costs.

8.8
How to Identify When You Are Being Catfished?

The likelihood of running into online fraud rises along with the popularity of online buying. It's crucial to always safeguard yourself, but what measures work best?

Shop at Reliable Websites

Beware of sketchy individuals who set up phoney online shops to take advantage of eager and trusting Christmas shoppers. Regardless of how well-known or obscure the online store is, always consider your options before clicking and handing over your money.

Use your computer browser to go directly to an online retailer instead of clicking a link in an email or social media post.

Read the comments to find out what other people think of a store's social media advertisements.

Search for the retailer, its online store, and its products to check reviews.

Look for any Facebook groups founded by dissatisfied clients.

Over the holiday season, make sure to keep an eye out for any unexpected activity on your bank statements. If you have any concerns that you may have fallen victim to fraud, contact your bank right once.

Secure Your Accounts

When you need to set up accounts with online stores, use unique, strong passwords rather than reusing your social network login information or your internet banking email address. Some online retailers may also demand a unique verification code provided to you via a different manner in addition to a username and password to protect your account when you make a purchase.

Check the Security of Your Payment

When completing a transaction on a shopping website, the URL (address) should always start with "https" and display a closed padlock icon in the address box. This shows that the communication between the shopping site and your device is encrypted (unable to be easily intercepted or read). Additionally, you might want to reconsider keeping your credit card information and other personal information on your online store accounts because, in the event of a breach, your information might fall into the hands of cybercriminals.

How to Protect Your Privacy on Social Media?

Privacy on social media is practically an oxymoron. Social media is public by definition. It connects people all around the world and offers a practical arena for knowledge sharing. However, it's best to keep some information secret.

There are steps you can do to improve your privacy if you enjoy socializing on social media but do not want to subject yourself to predators and dangerous online actors. You can modify your social media privacy in the following ways:

Read the Privacy Terms Carefully

There are privacy policies on every website on the internet, including social networking sites. All social media platforms' privacy policies should be reviewed and understood before making an account and logging in. Pay special attention to the privacy regulations governing the information you are registering and consenting to divulge when setting up an account on a social networking site. Examples include what information can be shared with others and whether or not the information on your website can be permanently removed.

Change the Privacy Settings

Before utilizing any social networking site, check its default privacy settings. The majority of social media sites' default privacy settings might make your information visible to other internet users.

Check Site Features

Make sure you are familiar with the features of the social networking site before broadcasting or posting any messages.

Determine whether all users of the platform will be able to see your communications or just a select group of people.

Biographical Information

Providing your biographical information, such as your complete name, birth date, age, or residence, is a requirement for creating an account on many social media sites.

Keep these details to yourself to minimize what other social media users know about you. Such details can provide cybercriminals with enough information to harm you.

Keep Your Location Off

When changing your privacy settings on your device, never forget to turn off location sharing.

By doing this, you can avoid reviewing places you frequently visit. If you disable your location, all of your emails, Facebook posts, and phone lookups are blocked.

What to Have Fun on the Internet and Be Safe?

There is a limitless amount of entertainment on the internet, making it difficult to become bored. Basically, going to the movies or reading publications are no longer the only options for amusement, thanks to the internet.

Play Games

There are plenty of free online games available, whether you prefer to play with a friend or by yourself. The nicest thing about these games is that there is nothing to download, which is perfect if you're using a school computer. There are 45 free games on "Flash by Night" that you may play by yourself in your web browser.

The focus of "Addicting Games" is, well, addictive games! Many different single-player and multiplayer games are available, including adventure, sports, and puzzle games.

Find a Fresh Webcomic.

There are a ton of fantastic digital comics to check out. Check out Penny Arcade, a seasoned webcomic that focuses on gaming culture if you're into gaming. You should also check out False Knees, xkcd, What's Up Beanie?, Cryptid Club, and Sarah's Scribbles, which are all excellent webcomics.

Listen to a Podcast

There are tens of thousands of podcasts available, so you'll never get bored. You can listen to podcasts using Google Podcasts, Spotify, or Mac's Podcasts.

Use Spotify, Google Podcasts, Pocket Casts, and the Podcasts app for iPad and iPhone to listen to your podcasts when you're on the go.

Use Music-Making Tools

With these entertaining Google-developed music-making tools, you can play a shared virtual piano, make rhythms, transform your voice, and more. Music Lab was created to make learning music available to everyone. You may use it to create melodies, experiment with oscillators, learn piano chords, and even generate rhythms using various drum sounds.

Watch Wildlife Cams

The best method to pass the time is to watch wildlife cams. There are sometimes built-in chats for viewers on animal-focused webcams, so you may participate and perhaps even meet new people. If you're lucky, you might witness a panda bear cuddling session or observe an eagle hatch from its egg.

Mangolinkcam is a hub for wildlife cameras from around the world, including those of insects, birds, African wildlife and marine life.

Numerous live-streaming cameras from sanctuaries, zoos, and wildlife reserves throughout the world can be found on Earthcam.

Happy Browsing!

Do You Remember?

- How can you check if your internet connection is secure?
- How can you check if a link is safe?
- What are some signs of an online predator?
- How can you make sure your account is safe while online shopping?
- Why do you need to keep your location off social sites?
- How can you enjoy the internet?

Roadmap for a Happy Life

Having fun and hanging out with friends is usually what teens are thinking about, so learning life skills is probably the last thing on your mind. But to live a happy, healthy life and overcome problems as an adult, having a strong set of life skills is crucial. You need to take the time to learn these crucial skills because they aren't always taught in school, including how to use public transportation, cook, and manage money. There are numerous advantages to developing these abilities as early as possible.

Learning life skills will help you develop social-emotional learning abilities, including social awareness, responsible decision-making, self-awareness, self-management, and the ability to form and maintain relationships and independence. Life skills help you with the capacity to think and solve problems in novel ways and understand the effects of your acts, which encourages you to take responsibility for your actions rather than place blame and gaining confidence in your speaking abilities also makes it much easier for you to communicate in groups.

It also helps with the ability to consider all of their options, come to decisions, and comprehend why they choose various courses of action. All of this increases one's awareness of oneself, appreciation for others and boosts flexibility.

Growing up presents its own unique problems and wonders. A teenager may not always be ready to live independently despite their age.

You need to be aware of a wide range of skills, including washing laundry, keeping a bank account, and paying taxes, and this is what this book is all about.

This life skills book is a comprehensive guide to lead you not only towards happy adulthood but also to ensure the healthiest teenage life. The book is divided into eight parts covering diverse subjects, from loving your imperfections to cooking to buying and driving your own car.

If you liked this book, please leave a review on Amazon.